GW00514692

EDITORIAL
Editor Maxwell Cooter
Managing Editor Marc Beishon
Design & Layout Heather Reeves
Contributors Adrian Bridgwater,
Dave Cartwright, Graham Jarvis, Billy
MacInnes, Lesley Meall

LICENSING & SYNDICATION
Licensing Hannah Heagney,
hannah_heagney@dennis.co.uk,
+44 20 7907 6134
Syndication Anj Dosaj-Halai,
Anj_Dosaj-Halai@dennis.co.uk,
+44 20 7907 6132

ADVERTISING & MARKETING
Advertising Manager
Ben Topp +44 20 7907 6625
MagBook Account Manager
Katie Wood +44 20 7907 6689
Digital Production Manager
Nicky Baker +44 20 7907 6056
Marketing & Editorial Executive
Emily Hodges +44 20 7907 6270

MANAGEMENT +44 20 7907 6000
MagBook Publisher Dharmesh Mistry
Publishing Director Jon Westnedge
Managing Director John Garewal
Deputy Managing Director Tim Danton
MD of Advertising Julian Lloyd-Evans
Newstrade Director David Barker
Chief Operating Officer Brett Reynolds
Group Finance Director Ian Leggett
Chief Executive James Tye
Chairman Felix Dennis

Printed by Stones

The Ultimate Guide To Cloud Computing
ISBN 9781907779831

We

Welcome to the *Ultimate Guide to Cloud Computing* – your indispensable reference point to all things cloud

YOU'VE PROBABLY PICKED UP this book because you've come across the term cloud computing and heard that it's going to be the dominant platform for delivering computing resources in the future. Research company IDC estimates that worldwide cloud market expenditure will be more than $70bn by 2015 – that's a 25% annual growth rate.

Over the following pages, you will read about what cloud computing is, what applications can run in the cloud (and what can't), how it can streamline your costs and how it will change your organisation – be that a major enterprise or a small business. You'll see how cloud will have an impact on all aspects of business life, from sales and marketing to managing a supply chain. And you'll read about the downsides too: from handling security to managing contracts, licensing and breakdowns in service.

We're set for a huge change in the way companies operate. The parallel that is often drawn is with the electricity supply and how we moved from a position where companies operated their own local power stations to using a national grid. It's an apt parallel but it doesn't go far enough – changing the source of the electricity supply didn't fundamentally change the way that businesses were run – cloud will.

The notion of offices in various locations supported by a dedicated IT team is going to slowly disappear. What the office of the future will look like is anyone's guess, but there is one guarantee – it will be served by some form of cloud computing.

The future starts here.

Maxwell Cooter, Editor

Contents

INSIDE

12

43

54

30

76

What is cloud?

Maxwell Cooter introduces the hot topic of cloud computing: what is it and where did it come from?

IT'S THE BUZZWORD on everybody's lips but what does cloud computing actually mean? It's not been an easy term to define and there have been many different attempts to explain what the term means. Cloud companies have been prone, like Alice's White Knight, to define the term in a way that they want it to mean.

In some ways it's strange that the term has been so slippery. Millions of us are happy to use such cloud-based services as Facebook, Gmail and Twitter, thinking nothing of it, yet pinning down an exact definition has been as elusive as grabbing a cloud itself.

In an attempt to put a stop to these vagaries, the US National Institute of Standards and Technology put forward a definition that has now become widely accepted as the closest that the industry has to a definitive answer. The NIST definition is as follows.

"Cloud computing is a model for enabling, convenient, on-demand network access to a shared pool of configurable computing resources (eg. networks, servers, storage, applications, and services) that can be rapidly provisioned and released with minimal management effort or service provider interaction. This cloud model promotes availability and is composed of five essential characteristics, three service models, and four deployment models."

The service models are types of offering, such as software-as-a-service (SaaS), and deployment choices include public and private clouds. But the key characteristics of cloud from a customer's point of view are:

- Self-provisioning so a customer can provision facilities without any human interaction
- Delivery of services over a network
- Ability to be accessed by a variety of devices, not just PCs but also by netbooks, tablet computers and smartphones
- Rapid 'elasticity' – the ability to scale up or scale down computing resources. From a cloud provider's point of view, a major element of the process is the pooling of computing resources to serve multiple consumers, using what's called a multi-tenant model whereby cloud services are provided to customers as and when they're needed. One of the important factors for cloud service providers is to be able to measure usage accurately and, even more importantly, to bill accurately.

Security concerns

The factor in cloud services that makes most users nervous is the level of security within a multi-tenant model. This is a major concern. Customers are entrusting some of their sensitive data to a third party and there is, ofcourse, nothing stopping one of their major competitors going to the same cloud provider for a service.

Service providers believe that this concern can be easily dealt with: they've generally had a long history of keeping customers data safe and have levels of security that far exceed those of their customers. Take Amazon, one of the

Difference between outsourcing and cloud computing

Outsourcing is widely known and used in technology circles. It's when a third party performs an IT function or other service on behalf of its customer. Outsourcing can be employed for a variety of reasons – lack of expertise in-house, lack of personnel or because the resources are needed purely for an individual project.

The key differences with cloud are defined by the underlying technology of the cloud provider. Essential to this is the use of virtualisation – all cloud providers make use of virtualisation technology – and automation (the ideal cloud service has little human intervention). The other key element of cloud computing is the use of self-provisioning – one of the major benefits is the ability to make a business more agile and flexible because services can be turned up and down at will.

leading lights in cloud technology. Millions of us around the world are willing to entrust our personal details and credit cards to that company believing they'll be held safely – why should trusting the company's cloud division, Amazon Web Services, be any different?

In many ways, a more important consideration than security is the location of the data. This is for two reasons. First, there is the inherent latency within the system: the further away the data is stored the longer the lag in accessing it. This is becoming less of a problem as network connection get faster but it still can be a factor.

The second problem is a more serious one, particularly on this side of the Atlantic. There are various EU regulations on where data can be stored – personal data cannot be held outside the EU (within the EU itself, individual countries have stricter guidelines still).

This has been a problem for some cloud providers, as part of the appeal is that unused resources at one data centre can be used by another. If data centres outside the EU cannot store European customers' data, providers have to be careful in marshalling their resources.

Allied to this is a secondary problem: the US Patriot Act, which compels US companies to hand over personal data held on their servers if requested by US authorities. As this applies to European data held on servers located in Europe, this has made some European customers rather nervous. The implications of the Patriot Act are still being worked through.

Virtual world

There are other elements within cloud computing. Virtualisation is another key concept. It means what it says, the use of virtual resources instead of physical ones. For example, a server within a data centre may be operating at just 15% of its capacity (this used to be a typical usage); virtualisation is a technique where the resources that aren't being used by the server for the application that it's driving (database, website or whatever) can be used for something else – driving usage rates up. Virtualisation will often go hand-in-hand with server consolidation so it helps to reduce the number of servers within a data centre.

A brief history of cloud computing

Anyone hanging around cloud vendors for any amount of time will hear one often repeated mantra – "Cloud computing is not new you know, cloud has been around for some time" – generally from a veteran of the technology industry. There's an element of truth in this but, at the same time, it's spectacularly missing the point.

It's possible to point to a 1966 book by Douglas Parkhill, *The Challenge of the Computer Utility*, for the origins of cloud computing. In that book, Parkhill detailed many of the elements of cloud computing – elastic provision, online delivery, perception of infinite supply – it's just taken a while for the theory to become reality.

Saying that the theories espoused in Parkhill's book are the first elements of cloud computing is a bit like saying that Leonardo Da Vinci's notebooks are the blueprints for the first helicopter. It's one thing coming forward with the theory, it's quite another delivering in practice. There have been plenty of false dawns before cloud computing became the beast it has become. We've seen it described as grid computing, computing on-demand and utility computing before the phrase cloud computing took hold. It's only been widely used since late 2007, although the term was first used in a lecture by computer scientist Ramnath Chellappa.

For cloud computing to become a reality, there were other changes needed first. Most important of these was the availability of fast and cheap broadband – the early attempts at cloud computing all foundered because of the dearth of such a service. Then virtualisation needed to become more widespread, as this technology is the bedrock of cloud computing.

Other factors are the declining cost in storage, the availability of cheaper devices to access cloud services and the development of automatic provisioning software.

Like cloud computing, it's an old concept, originating from the mainframe world and only becoming widely used after VMware, a virtualisation specialist, started applying it to servers. The technology has now been adopted nearly universally within enterprises and the technique of re-allocating resources has made it vital for the development of the cloud.

We've spoken a lot about cloud service providers but another important part of the cloud is the delivery of software – the so-called software-as-a-service (SaaS) delivery mechanism. This is a technique that was really pioneered by Salesforce.com with its hosted CRM product but has since been adopted by countless other companies. SaaS delivery helps solve various problems within an enterprise: over-provisioning, security updates and licensing among them, and is widely seen now as the dominant method for providing software.

As a concept, cloud computing has grown quickly and is set to penetrate deeper into the market. According to an oft-cited Gartner report, 20% of enterprises will have no IT departments by the end of 2012. While that looks to be a bit optimistic (or pessimistic depending on your view), the impetus is clearly with cloud. It's a technology that's here to stay. ■

Which way is cloud moving?

Marc Beishon looks in detail at cloud models and where the action is in the consumer and business sectors

IT IS CERTAINLY TRUE that many people, particularly in business, would like a clear definition of cloud computing. As a report and survey from industry body CompTIA, 'Cloud computing: pulling back the curtain', says, both the industry and end user communities "crave a more authoritative, uniform definition of cloud computing to help them determine how best to exploit it from a business and technology perspective".

It too points to the definition from the National Institute of Standards and Technology (NIST), as discussed on page 7, and it is worth adding the full list of characteristics and models in the definition (see also the glossary, page 96 for explanations of most of these terms):

Essential characteristics
- On-demand self-service
- Broad network access
- Resource pooling
- Rapid elasticity
- Measured service

Service models
- Software-as-a-service (SaaS)
- Platform-as-a-service (PaaS)
- Infrastructure-as-a-service (IaaS)

Deployment models
- Public cloud
- Private cloud
- Hybrid cloud
- Community cloud

The NIST model has the benefit of simplicity, but inevitably there are many more detailed attributes of cloud services that are confusing people, which is not surprising at this early stage of the evolution of cloud computing. But users in organisations are starting to form a consensus on what they 'strongly associate' the cloud with, says CompTIA, namely 'offsite', 'Internet centric', 'shared', 'scalable', 'software-as-a-service' and 'virtualised resource'.

What is not confusing is the sheer scale of the projections for the size of the cloud computing market, as the analysts are all agreed that, definitions aside, users will be voting with their feet and fuelling a global market worth more than £100bn by 2013 with a major component being the use of cloud software applications such as those from Google and Salesforce.com, the customer relationship management specialist. One analyst, Gartner, has predicted that 20% of all businesses will own no IT infrastructure by 2012, and will be virtually total cloud users.

That's particularly true for smaller companies and start-ups, as the kind of cloud services they can use to run operations are similar to those that have gained rapid ground in consumer markets. Sole traders, small companies and also hobbyists and casual users are

all making great use of cloud platforms such as eBay, Amazon and PayPal to conduct day-to-day business with nothing more than a laptop, Internet connection and a bank account.

Cloud for consumers

And even a smartphone or tablet will do – the cloud services that will dominate in the consumer market are mobile applications, driven by the huge success of products such as Apple's iPhone and iPad, and the Android standard adopted by other handset players. News that created much interest in August 2011 was the proposed buy-up of Motorola's

Mobility handset business by Google, which points in one direction only – that of a near future where huge public cloud applications such as those of Google will be seamlessly available on your smartphone wherever you go.

It is no surprise that Apple, meanwhile, planned to launch in autumn 2011 its iCloud – "cloud service done right", as the giant firm says. iCloud is a replacement for Apple's previous cloud efforts, but clearly the company now feels confident to pitch its offering badged as a cloud service ('MobileMe' was the main earlier version for productivity applications). It has now brought together all its online services – productivity such as mail and contacts, the iTunes media store, online backup and storage, and access to new applications – in one cloud that services users automatically as they move around (in a so-called 'push' way).

It's also free to Apple customers, in the same way that people can already make use of free mail and considerable amounts of storage with services such as Hotmail, Yahoo and Google. Apple – which briefly became the world's largest company in August 2011 – is great at engineering an almost fanatical user experience, and it rarely gets its marketing wrong these days, so the ubiquity of a personal computing and media cloud is likely to be taken for granted by many in the next few years.

What the company will have to rely on though is a large network of partners to deliver its experience, especially the mobile phone operators and their many suppliers of base station equipment, transmission technology and customer provisioning and billing systems. Experience of the mobile cloud, in particular, can be easily scuppered if you can't get a signal at a vital moment, or you get a massive unexpected bill, and it's no surprise that poor customer service is now to the fore as people migrate into increasing use of mobile data and cloud services.

Mobile data applications and services are set to drive the growth of consumer cloud services

That mobility is the key consumer cloud area is borne out by research firm Business Insights, which predicts that mobile applications will make up almost half of the market for revenues by 2018. "Mobile applications and services are set to drive the growth of consumer cloud services, as consumers demand 'always-on' and ubiquitous access to data, entertainment and services," it says. Next, and as some may not be surprised to hear, is online gaming, followed by 'voice over IP' (ie Internet telephony services such as Skype), and paid music content. In terms of revenues, services such as email and online storage barely figure, as they look set to remain free or very low cost.

Cloud for business

Patterns of use for companies and organisations in the public and third sectors are also becoming apparent, with CompTIA, for example, noting that a 'sweet spot' for cloud adoption is in the medium sized company sector (say between £10m and £100m in turnover). This is because they have similar IT needs to large enterprises, but less cash for on-premise systems, and so can deploy cloud computing instead as an operational expense with a more predictable cost model.

Reducing capital expenditure and other costs is often the number one reason for moving to cloud computing, but coming in second is the desire to add new capabilities that just aren't available otherwise, and this key factor must surely rise to the top as more organisations discover just how transformational the cloud can be for business processes. Indeed, in another survey of SMEs alone, the benefit of expanding capabilities does come out ahead of cost savings.

Other factors for deploying cloud are the speed with which it can be rolled out, simplicity, subscription pricing, an end to conventional software licensing, and lower energy use. Pertinently, cutting internal IT staff, while a factor for some, is not a major reason for cloud, suggesting that these workers may be better deployed on IT activities that really help the business rather than traditional IT pursuits such as 'firefighting'.

The type of service that companies are mostly deploying are software-as-a-service (SaaS) offerings – in CompTIA's survey, of those using the cloud 69% have a SaaS product in use, 31% IaaS and 22% PaaS, although the latter two may well be part of a SaaS solution in a managed service provider's data centre.

Indeed, a majority of user organisations plan to source their cloud computing from a third party provider, above self-service/direct from the Internet, or direct from a technology vendor, suggesting that there is plenty of scope still for skilled IT providers that can add value, say, by packaging cloud software into private clouds for superior and more secure service.

As far as types of provider go, there are various models that include:

- Public cloud provider with own data centre
- Private cloud specialist working with customers to build internal clouds
- Hybrid provider of private and public clouds hosted in own or third-party data centre
- Reseller of cloud services (eg. SaaS).

Going it alone

But of course there is nothing stopping any organisation signing up direct with a cloud software player such as Salesforce.com, although it may be wise to employ a consultancy that can adapt the company's business processes to work with the cloud offering, as it will rarely be the case that it will go smoothly 'out of the box' – there will be set-up operations that need to be carried out.

As for the applications and services that companies are taking up in the cloud, there are certain offerings that are

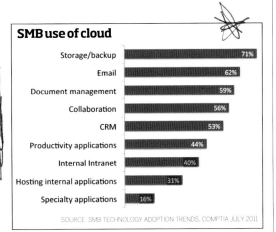

SMB use of cloud

Storage/backup	71%
Email	62%
Document management	59%
Collaboration	56%
CRM	53%
Productivity applications	44%
Internal Intranet	40%
Hosting internal applications	31%
Specialty applications	16%

SOURCE: SMB TECHNOLOGY ADOPTION TRENDS, COMPTIA JULY 2011

ahead of the pack, in particular storage and backup, and email (see also above from an SMB – small and medium sized business – survey). Storage is one of the most widely offered cloud services, which is not surprising given its relative simplicity and value in providing offsite peace of mind for data. Most firms will have taken up cloud storage and backup in some form in the next few years.

Email too is pretty much standard as a cloud service now, and is often coupled with value-added extras such as spam and virus management. Indeed, security services on the Internet is a class of cloud offering in its own right and one that has been a big growth area for specialist providers. Extra security measures and policies are vital when moving to public cloud services, in particular.

Other applications are less popular right now for the cloud – CRM though, as pioneered by Salesforce.com is a favourite, and others such as document management and collaboration have strong showings. Content management generally – as organisations do battle with growing disparate data mountains, and increasingly mobile workforces – is clearly a winner for the cloud. ∎

Are you afraid of
cloud computing?

Cloud computing offers clear benefits to many
organisations, but like any new technology concept there
are reservations about being an 'early adopter'.
Simon Brew finds out if these fears are real

CLOUD COMPUTING ISN'T REALLY a
new idea that's just sprung up over
the past few months. Rather, it's the
summation of a series of technologies
that have been converging for some
time. Now, cloud computing has
become a solid option for

organisations of all sizes – so what's
holding them back?

Plenty, as it happens. Here, we
take a look at ten of the main reasons
people might be holding back on
deploying cloud-based working, and
how valid they are.

▶

1 Infrastructure

A clear requirement for effective cloud working is fast, reliable Internet access, especially for smaller organisations that are using public cloud providers. You need enough bandwidth so that those who need to collaborate and work across cloud technologies are able to do so. That's something that's quite easy to manage when the bulk of workers are in an office – provided the Internet connection is up – but it gets trickier with remote workers and those who travel.

Regular travellers will be aware of the difficulty of finding a workable, secure web connection. And given that one of the main benefits of cloud working is to have access to files and applications wherever you happen to be, variable web access quality has to be a concern.

This of course applies equally to people accessing in-house computers over the Internet. But when everyone in an organisation is dependent on a cloud platform, there is an understandable concern that there is no fall-back position for a vital part of a company's infrastructure – and one that underpins most other operations now.

2 Losing control of data

It's not just an emotional attachment to a computer room that keeps companies from outsourcing data. It's the fact that there's an inherent feeling of security in having data under close control (assuming there's some kind of remote backup for disaster recovery, of course).

Removing the need for local storage clearly has some cost benefits, but for a generation of system administrators and support staff brought up on a different way of working, it's a change that rings some alarm bells.

One in particular is trusting an external source for working data – what happens if access drops or if someone loses the data? Even appreciating the security that cloud computing offers, there's a leap of faith and an element of uncertainty (along with a loss of transparency), that creeps in when data management is moved out of the immediate control of an IT department.

3

Fear of change

People do fear any sort of change, even in a fast moving industry such as IT. They don't tend to fear upgrades too much – although a jump say to the latest Microsoft Office can mean some firefighting – but a wholesale alteration in the way systems are supposed to work is a challenge.

It's hard not to have some sympathy with this. In many organisations, IT is a tool, a means to do a job, and nothing more than that. There's a strong argument that the software industry, in particular, has become adept at selling upgrades and alterations that we don't actually need, or that don't make a difference to daily life. So when a change comes along that does, reticence is hardly surprising.

Persuading people to alter the way that they've done things for years, whether attempted via carrot or stick, is rarely a straightforward battle.

So persuading key decision makers and their staff to embrace cloud computing can be a heck of a job in and of itself. Even the best-deployed cloud solution might therefore still be a bit of a bumpy ride (see also number 10 – the human factor).

4

Security

When data is being looked after by another party, it's right and proper that security issues are raised. Every business has confidential information that it likes to keep behind closed doors, and the fear that cloud computing could make such material more vulnerable isn't one that can simply be ignored.

Yet recent times have seen that the biggest source of confidential document leaks is more likely to have been a misplaced USB stick, using unsecured Internet connections and less than honest employees.

Reputable cloud service providers view security as pivotal to what they offer and, with the added help of a bit of common sense, there's a strong argument that most businesses would benefit from more robust security if they do migrate to a cloud service.

5

Cloud outage

Clearly, this is a very real and sensible concern. There's no computer network in the world that doesn't have the risk of downtime at some point in its life. However, there's still the comfort blanket of being able to yell at an IT department and get up-to-the-minute information when it's a self-hosted computer network that's at the heart of the problem.

What happens, though, when that's taken out into a cloud environment? Who gets the ear-bashing then? And, more to the point, what happens when a cloud service a business is relying on goes down, even for a short period? With localised working, even without a network, having some machines with working productivity software installed at least means things can get done.

What's often forgotten in this argument, though, is that a cloud service stands a good chance of having a working, operational backup called into action quickly. Furthermore, one by-product of cloud adoption is that the maintenance and repair of problems is also outsourced, so it may well be that any problems are resolved faster than an in-house team can act.

Service providers should – and do – also have incentives to ensure maximum uptime.

6

Paying the bill

There are some obvious economic benefits to adopting cloud services, from a reduction in dependency on in-house IT, to the outsourcing of data management and security, and the saving, potentially, on expensive software licences, and battling to keeping hardware performance up to date.

Yet the future is uncertain. Technology is littered with examples of new innovations and developments that were initially designed to reduce costs, and yet many business are still investing heavily in their IT budgets.

Some valid questions arise about cloud computing, then. Is it offering value for money? What guarantees are in place that pricing won't slide upwards as businesses become more and more dependant on cloud services? Is this just software companies trying to get us to switch to a subscription system for licences, and so the longer term cost may actually be higher?

These are appropriate questions, often with no immediate answer. There's an element of leap of faith, and a need to down a good service contract. But cast iron guarantees? They're lacking at present, and for firms with razor-tight balance sheets that has to be an issue.

7

It's too early

Even accepting the comparable maturity of some elements of cloud-based working (many, for instance, trust their email to a webmail service with little worry), there remains a feeling, rightly or wrongly, that this is still an area of computing that's in its infancy. Let's not forget, too, that lots of 'next big things' have gone on to be anything but. As such, many businesses are holding back from adopting cloud services as they wait to see how the assorted offerings develop, and as they let others do the pathfinding for them.

There's always some sense to not moving business-critical operations to areas where you'd be an early adopter (although cloud adoption can, and should, be done piecemeal), and there's a feeling that the wrinkles need to be resolved in cloud services before more firms embrace the potential on offer.

Yet, there's a degree of obvious myth to the argument that the services are immature – after all, Saleforce.com has been around since 1999, an eternity in IT terms. Rather, we are more likely reacting to changes in the way services are packaged and sold, although there are clear reasons to be cautious if, say, the local Internet infrastructure is rather poor and you want to invest in a public cloud system.

8

We are not lemmings

Much of the discussion surrounding cloud computing has implicit assumptions built into it. That it's the right thing to do. That it's the logical next step in business technology. That it's a question of when, rather than if, a company should take advantage of what cloud computing offers. In much the same way that it was once assumed that everybody would upgrade their copy of Windows within a couple of years of Microsoft releasing a new version, there's an impression sometimes put across that cloud computing will become compulsory.

But, of course, it isn't. There is doubt that the argument that cloud is the future has been convincingly made. Because, while there are potentially huge benefits to what's being offered, there's no one-size-fits-all mentality here. Is cloud computing really the right option for a small business of two or three people? Is it the right way forward for a large organisation, with hundreds of employees in many different locations?

There are strong cases to be made in both instances that the answer is yes (again, down to the fact that you can choose what works for you, with public, private and hybrid cloud approaches on offer). But that doesn't mean that the case doesn't have to be made.

The benefits of the cloud have to be defined, be tangible, and be presented properly. It's the users who tumble over the cliff to follow the crowd who will, inevitably, hit problems, and fail to reap the intended benefits of what the cloud can offer.

▶

9

What, actually, is it?

Arguably one of the biggest challenges facing cloud computing is this: how, exactly, do you define it? Because already, different service providers describe cloud products in very different ways. There doesn't appear to be one widely accepted definition of what cloud computing is, and without that, packaging and selling the benefits to organisations is made that bit more difficult.

Furthermore, part and parcel of the uncertainties surrounding cloud computing is the argument over standards. There's no solid, common and obvious foundation for cloud services to build on. Like it or lump it, people know where they are with a Windows operating system, a copy of Lotus Notes and some variant of an office suite. But what such common, unifying tools exist in the cloud? There are not, at this stage, obvious, dominant players in the market – although Amazon, Google and Salesforce.com would stake claims – and for companies looking for a big brand name to trust, that does have to come into their thinking.

Until cloud computing can be defined in a manner that's as understandable as an operating system or an office suite (and arguably, it can be defined as both), it's going to create some uncertainty within firms as to what exactly they're being sold, and how it allows them to work with others.

10

The human factor

At the heart of every significant problem to do with technology lies the same factor: people. We have seen time and time again that you can have an IT infrastructure that's seemingly tight and secure, but it's a simple human slip that's opened up an element of risk. Furthermore, someone who doesn't fully understand, or doesn't want to understand, what it is that they're being presented with, will always cause some degree of problem.

It may be straightforward to get the MD and finance director to sign off on the financial benefits, but just look at how hard it is to get 'buy-in' for end users to use systems such as CRM (customer relationship management). New web-based systems in the cloud may pose similar problems.

Realistically, of course, every issue we've discussed here has a person at the heart of it, or a fear of what someone can and inevitably will do when given the keys to something new and different (and that's just one individual: the potential dangers multiply exponentially when people hunt in packs).

It's a big problem, and why many businesses are keen to retain the technological status quo, in that it keeps the human–technology balance in a position that it's migrated to over a period of time.

It's important never to forget the 'people factor' when bringing in any new technology ∎

Microsoft Global Hosting
Partner of the Year 2011

99.99%
NETWORK UPTIME †

BOOST BUSINESS WITH A
VIRTUAL
SERVER

BEST UK SPEC

Maximise performance and uptime

Respond faster to the changing needs of your business with a virtual server from Fasthosts. You'll get a cost-effective, dedicated resource that you can easily expand. A virtual server is ideal if you need to run business-critical applications or busy websites.

You'll get better performance and uptime from our award-winning Microsoft Hyper-V platform, which provides load-balancing and automatic failover. To find out more about this technology and why our virtual servers offer the best spec in the UK, visit:
www.fasthosts.co.uk/why-we-are-better.

Microsoft | Hyper-V Cloud

Award Winner 2011
INDUSTRY LEADING TECHNOLOGY FOR OVER 10 YEARS

Powered by
DELL · Windows Server 2008 R2 · SQL Server 2008 · Parallels Plesk Panel

From just:
£29.99
per month ex VAT

24/7 UK phone & online support · UK data centres · Unlimited bandwidth* · FREE setup

Call us now on:
0844 692 3519
fasthosts.co.uk/virtualservers

fasthosts ™
World Class Virtual Servers

Microsoft Partner Network™

2011 PARTNER OF THE YEAR
Hosting
Winner

Microsoft
GOLD CERTIFIED
Partner

Follow us on:

How the cloud can make your business agile

This talk of technology is all very well, but the cloud's true potential is in transforming your business with speed and collaboration, as **Marc Beishon** finds out

HANDS UP WHO remembers timesharing computers in universities? Or value-added networks (VANs) and electronic data interchange (EDI) in business trading networks? Or Prudential salespeople armed with Psion palmtop computers?

Many proponents of cloud computing act as though they've just discovered the kind of cloud-type business processes that organisations have, in fact, been tackling with various degrees of success for many years. These advocates also maintain that cloud is a technology-driven new wave that, while bringing new business opportunities, is mainly about scaling up infrastructure in data centres, with the obvious advantages of access to latest technology, elimination of in-house servers and so on.

But the technology itself, while obviously vital, is really a sideshow to realising the business transformation efforts that enlightened organisations have been striving for over the last 20 years or so. As Walter Adamson, an Australian-based consultant, comments:

"Clouds are about ecosystems, about large collections of interacting services including partners and third parties, about inter-cloud communication and sharing of information through such semantic frameworks as social graphs."

Transformation vs utility

This, he adds, is clearly business transformational, whereas "computing services that are delivered as a utility from a remote data centre" are not. The pioneers in VANS/EDI methods – which are now migrating into modern cloud systems in offerings from software firm SAP and its partners, for example – were able to set up basic trading data exchange networks, but the cloud transformation now is integrating, in real-time, the procurement, catalogue, invoicing and other systems across possibly overlapping and much wider business communities.

Likewise, companies struggled for a

long time with mobile and remote access to sales and marketing systems, as enterprise integration was often very difficult and expensive. Now the transformation brought about by cloud ecosystems such as the Salesforce.com community is enabling far more than a mobile quotation system with data that a rep had to download using a modem before he or she set out for the day.

And clearly, there are many individuals and companies, especially small firms, that have happily taken to one of the world's most complete cloud experiences, Amazon Web Services, which is enabling many to move from a static website to a fully-fledged online global shop, with everything from database management to micropayment handling. And Amazon is also a frontrunner in the enterprise 'private cloud', with major software vendors – including Oracle and SAP – now on its infrastructure offering.

But is that offering business agility beyond the IT side? A recent *Business Week* article, 'The cloud: battle of the tech titans', looks at Amazon vs the rest and focuses pretty much on the scale argument, with users renting server time to analyse sales data, for example. But it does note that time to market is a major pull.

The city of Miami, for example, has quickly built a service that monitors non-emergency calls. "Local residents can go to a website that pulls up a map of the city and place pins in every spot tied to a complaint. Before the cloud, the city would have needed three months to develop a concept, buy new computing systems (including extras in case of a hurricane), get a team to install all the necessary software, and then build the service." Such systems are unlikely to be built in the 'conventional' way in these cash-strapped days.

Sandwich course

Good use of a private cloud – this time on Google Apps – is by food chain EAT, which is improving business processes by using Google Talk for instant messages between stores when one run outs of a popular sandwich, for instance; Google Forms for head office to survey shop managers to capture issues and ideas; and integration with smartphones, for managers to access documents and order stocks on the move, and to oversee a number of restaurants while being stationed at one.

The received wisdom about such business cloud applications is that vendors are approaching business department heads, not IT managers, to make sales, although not much enterprise software of any type has been sold this way since the dot-com crash.

It certainly makes sense in one of the ▶

hardest functions to crack, the salesforce, which has long put up resistance to clunky CRM (customer relationship management) systems foisted on them. Just because Salesforce.com's CRM system is cloud-based does not mean it does not have the adoption problems that CRM has suffered from – incentives and good management tend to fix that. But a cloud system can greatly help with business change in hard to reach parts of a firm.

In many companies there is a black hole of forecasting and pipeline data on sales, and it doesn't help that most major enterprises – certainly in the FTSE 100 – are led by CEOs with no sales experience. It's an area tailor-made for the cloud since so much knowledge is in silos – around departments and in the heads of salespeople – and best practice is not shared.

Fast forward for sales

Phil Codd, chief markets officer for northern Europe at software testing firm SQS, chose Salesforce.com to solve a major sales reporting problem – in the past, reporting was on an individual country basis with a complex mix of spreadsheets, emails and word of mouth which placed a lot of pressure on accurate and timely sales forecasting.

Codd took advantage of Salesforce. com's 30 day free trial of its Sales Cloud 2, and then worked with consultancy SaasPoint to implement it in just 40 working days – and the company now has a central repository of sales pipeline throughout the region in real-time, and all sorts of new opportunities for sharing sales best practice and leads by using tools such as Salesforce.com's Chatter, an internal social media system.

Anything that produces more than the sum of a notoriously self-sufficient group

of reps is more than useful and it's hard to underestimate what this can do for a company – Larry Ellison, the colourful boss of software giant Oracle and now a cloud convert, famously cracked the whip a few years ago when he realised he had no 'dashboard' to see what his business units were doing in a timely fashion round the world – and got it done, of course.

In-house not an option

Trying to build an in-house systems to do this is obviously counter-productive in time and money for most companies that are not of the likes of Oracle. And where Salesforce.com also scores is in its brilliant decision to create the AppExchange platform where users can integrate and use many more functions, from an 800 long list, and that's apart from Salesforce's own extras.

Another function that's benefiting from cloud 'agility' is logistics, where provider Deltion is gaining a good deal of success for its CarrierNet platform. Managing director Denis O'Sullivan, himself a logistics expert brought in to run this UK firm a year ago, says logisticians have been 'crying out' for a long time for real-time visibility across the supply chain to iron out customer service problems, which he says Cadbury (now part of Kraft) is doing with CarrierNet, a cloud system.

Keith Newton, customer logistics director at Cadbury says: "The implementation has enabled us to move from a series of unlinked systems to a web based interfaced solution that has totally eliminated a number of areas of failure. It links all internal logistics and planning teams at Cadbury, all tier one third party logistics service providers, all second tier hauliers subcontracted to them, and customers via alerts, SMS

More business applications in the cloud

- Human resources (HR) systems are not obvious targets for the cloud but vendors such as SuccessFactors are proving that properly managing the entire workforce in terms of skills, knowledge and structure can have a big impact on business performance. European users such as construction supplier Hilti are big fans.

- The public sector has much to gain from the cloud – in the NHS, County Durham and Darlington Foundation Trust, a consortium of ten organisations, is using Wax Digital's web3 procurement system to make it easier for staff across the consortium to select goods and services for purchase and place orders quickly and simply, enable streamlined financial control and authorisation, and accelerate the supply process to nearly always 'next day'.

- Project management is a shoo-in for the cloud, as Vodafone is discovering with the Projectplace web-based communication systems. "Finally we have a central system for storing files, working on them and retrieving them, always in real-time. Any project member can access it, and most importantly, the latest version is always available," says Alexander Gottschlich, global programme manager at Vodafone.

- The Green House, a small Northampton-based business specialising in environmental services, manages around 500,000 scheduled collections a year through its recycling division alone. In the past, all of these transactions would have been carried out manually. Issues were typically sorted out over the telephone with multiple calls routinely taking place between the company, its suppliers and clients. This was a time-consuming, resource-intensive and expensive process. Today, the company manages all of these collections through Salesforce.com's Service Cloud, into which it has integrated a large number of workflows and approval procedures.

and emails. "It is no coincidence that since implementation we have recorded a number of '100% customer service days', which is a significant achievement for a large FMCG firm such as Cadbury."

For which read – if the truck breaks down and no one knows, the kids don't get their chocolate. O'Sullivan adds that large retailers are also in the market for his system – which again would be prohibitive now to try and build in-house – and also mentions a client called Rigid Plastic Containers (RPC) which uses CarrierNet to check warehouse stock and production schedules before processing transport orders. If there is no warehouse stock, the system checks if the ordered items will be produced in time for despatch. If there is a potential problem, an exception alert is raised and the problem managed with the customer.

Logistics examples are significant because they often involve the ecosystems that promote more business transformation across partners – adding real-time bidding systems to take on jobs, for example, is another feature O'Sullivan mentions that a client is doing. An ecosystem also becomes apparent within companies as they use cloud systems for human resources.

In some cases, it is certainly the case that cloud technology creates a new business agility opportunity. In others, it's enabling better a known need. Donald Rumsfeld had a good take on this… ∎

Should you go private or public?

MUCH OF THE DEBATE about cloud computing has focused on two distinct types of operation: the public and private clouds. But although they are bundled under the convenient term of cloud computing, they are very different operational models.

Public started with Amazon

Public cloud, which is simply using the Internet to access computer services of one sort or another, has its roots in the decision by Amazon in 2002 to use its vast infrastructure to offer computer facilities to customers. The company launched a range of services to developers, including storage and a development platform.

Amazon's initiative, which preceded the phrase 'cloud computing' itself, has been followed by the likes of Google and a selection of hosting companies as they seek to capture the interest in this approach.

As if to demonstrate that there's nothing new under the sun, this is a throwback to the concept of the computer bureau, where companies paid a monthly fee to buy time on a mainframe. It's a business that had seemed to die a death when PCs and the client-server model came into play.

Like the computer bureaux, public cloud providers charge their customers on a monthly basis – generally according to gigabytes transmitted and bandwidth. The crucial aspect is that the cloud

It's not just a question of moving to the cloud; do you opt for a public or private system? **Maxwell Cooter** weighs up the options

provider bears the entire cost of running the infrastructure, meaning that as a customer you do not have to worry about maintenance or staffing help desks. Nor do you have to worry about investing in storage hardware, a growing budgetary strain on organisations as data storage volumes move ever upwards.

Crucially, it also means that you do not have to worry about capacity planning. This can be a big headache for companies with seasonal fluctuations, where they might have over-provisioned for peak traffic. That's a headache that the new breed of cloud providers can deal with.

So, public cloud offers a number of advantages to organisations, particularly small businesses and start-ups, both of which may have no IT department and which may be reluctant to tie up capital on an IT infrastructure. There are, however, downsides too.

The main disadvantage with public cloud is that there are some security issues. Companies will have to hand over confidential data over to a third party and for many firms this is a move too far. There will be worries about customer data being released into the public domain, concerns about companies being held legally responsible for breaches of privacy legislation and worries about sensitive data being held on a server, particularly where two competitors might be hosted.

But if you're starting small, public ▶

In the private cloud, you have responsibility for buying the hardware and software, maintaining it and managing storage

cloud will almost certainly be the way to go as it will be able to handle something as small as say a basic client contact database for a couple of salespeople. And many providers offer simple storage services for single users.

In control with private cloud

The genesis of the private cloud was very different. There's no public operator and everything – hardware and software – is provided by you, the user. It sounds little different from a more conventional data centre, where your servers and applications are hosted by a specialist provider. Indeed there are some commentators who claim that the idea of a private cloud is an oxymoron, and really we should be talking about data centres.

Proponents of private clouds maintain there is a difference: the main features of a private cloud are a 'virtualised' infrastructure coupled with software that allows IT users to treat that

infrastructure as a centralised pool of computing resources.

Other features of the private cloud are automation, meaning that many of these tasks are handled without the intervention of an IT department, and the ability to measure and monitor what resources have been allocated to different departments, which could also means companies are able to introduce chargeback for resources that have been consumed.

In the private cloud set-up, you have responsibility for buying the hardware and software, maintaining it and managing storage. As such, private cloud doesn't offer so many advantages when it comes to managing cash flow.

But there are other advantages. You connect to public cloud providers by using Internet connections – these are, by their very nature, slow. This means that anyone trying to shift large files around would find the experience a lot of slower. On the other hand, private

PUBLIC VS PRIVATE CLOUD: pros and cons

PUBLIC PROS
- Less expensive than private clouds
- More accessible than private clouds
- Short-term or temporary commitments
- Faster to deploy a single user than private clouds

PRIVATE PROS
- Can be secured to meet compliance at almost every level
- Single tenant environments eliminate the possibility of other companies affecting performance
- Private data centres usually accessible to IT auditors
- Customisable to meet an individual organisation's needs, rather than the mass approach of public clouds

PUBLIC CONS
- Fewer user management controls
- One-size-fits all approach (not tailored to a single organisation's or user's needs)
- Impersonal support, often via email, chat, or FAQs only
- Security and uptime might not meet enterprise compliance standards

PRIVATE CONS
- More expensive to deploy and maintain than public clouds
- May have longer-term commitments than public clouds
- May have less flexibility since hardware is dedicated to a single organisation

SOURCE: WWW.FOGODATACENTERS.COM

cloud infrastructures often use private connections, offering a much speedier experience, although there are issues for branch offices that may need to use a slower wide area network to get access to the main corporate link.

In addition, the private cloud doesn't have the security issues that could cause problems for public cloud users. All data is retained by your company and you control all access over a private 'firewall'.

What's important here is that not only do you keep tabs on data – but you also know exactly where, geographically speaking, it's being held. This not an academic principle, as there are important legal restraints on where data can or cannot be held and companies have to be wary of their statutory duty for protecting customer information.

Why not go hybrid?
There's no need to choose between private or public, as organisations with more than basic needs for cloud IT can opt for both in a hybrid approach, with some services in a private cloud, others in a public one. This could still be managed by one provider and can address concerns such as holding sensitive data – such as customer credit card details – only on a private basis.

But you may be quite happy for staff to use say Twitter or Facebook – which are public cloud applications, after all – for customer communication, or any of the Google apps, such as Calendar and Docs, or say Salesforce.com, for communications among groups of staff, where ease of use is the foremost consideration. ∎

Board-level
priorities for cloud

Maxwell Cooter takes a tour through the top board jobs affected by what for many will be a major business change in the years ahead

CLOUD COMPUTING HAS had a short history. It was unheard of as a term before 2007 and in just four years it has risen from marketing shorthand to become the symbol of a massive change in technology.

What makes cloud computing different is that it's a technological change that touches on every part of the business. For the finance director there are changes in the way IT services are bought; sales managers have a new way to communicate and interact with their teams and customers; the IT director will find his or her budget, strategy and team transformed. Above all, the CEO will have to think about the way his or her entire organisation is structured.

In the future, we could be talking about a complete overhaul of the way companies are constructed, about how they consume IT, about how their accounting works and, indeed, where they're located (see also section on business change, page 22).

But those changes mean different things to different parts of the business. If we look at the way cloud services impact on different job roles, we can see that they're going to approach these changes in very different ways.

For the finance director

Perhaps the biggest driver for the move to cloud is the need to save costs, but that move works on many levels.

The change that has garnered most publicity is the move from counting IT as a capital expenditure to an operational one. Although often cited as a reason to move from on-premise hosting to cloud, this is somewhat misleading. What's really at stake is cash flow; by going down the cloud route, customers no longer have to commit to large costs upfront. It isn't necessarily true to say ▶

that it's always going to be cheaper, but there are other advantages.

There may even be a price premium in opting for cloud, but that needs to be set aside for other considerations. The price of renting a server could initially appear to cost more than purchasing, but the finance director has to consider the cost of power and cooling, the cost of staff, the maintenance costs, accounting for backup and disaster recovery and various other costs.

There's also the fact there's no longer the need to be so rigorous about capacity planning – that becomes a headache for the cloud provider, not your IT director – and companies will be more flexible about installing new services and scaling up and down.

This is an important aspect. Previously the IT department would have installed an infrastructure that would be able to handle the peaks of the business. This was always a grossly inefficient way of organising IT services. It could be an infrastructure that is geared up to handle peaks of traffic – perhaps around the end of financial quarters, or around Christmas for retailers.

You no longer need to be so rigorous about capacity planning – that becomes a headache for the cloud provider, not your IT director

But those brief periods of intense activity would have an effect on IT provision for the entire year – rather as if a family of four opted for a minibus purely to cope with the yearly visit of the cousins who lived abroad. Cloud computing changes all that: for the first time, organisations will no longer have to plan for the periods of greatest demand.

Coupled with this will be a change of practice when it comes to allocating departmental costs. Finance directors will now have an accurate way of

deciding which costs are set against which department. This is a fundamental shake-up: even companies that have chargeback to separate departments have often found this is little more than an estimate of a share of the costs. Managers have few tools to assess a real cost and have derived a figure from a combination of real figures and informed guesses.

Now there's a real way of measuring just now much computing time the marketing department has used, how much storage the graphics department has grabbed and the bandwidth needs of finance.

That capability, however, could lead to some finely tuned judgment. When

vendors have not yet grasped the transformational nature of cloud computing and their licensing models are not able to cope with this new paradigm. The finance director, in conjunction with the IT head, needs to assess the state of licensing within the organisation, making sure that the company isn't overpaying.

The thorniest problem of all will be the negotiation and monitoring of the service level agreements (SLAs) with cloud providers. While the IT director will probably remain the best person to check on service delivery, the finance director will need some understanding of the potential level of financial loss suffered and the possible levels of compensation. This is a crucial area for the move to cloud computing: delivery to this sort of model will never work if the cloud provider can't provide the desired level of service and if the customer is under-compensated.

Ever since cloud computing emerged as a new catchphrase for the IT world, there have been several vendors leaping on to the cloud bandwagon and 'cloud washing' existing products to suggest a strong commitment to the cloud. There are some finance directors or IT directors who may be tempted to follow the same path and 'cloud wash' their IT department. These instances will probably be rare but there's certainly been some resistance to the idea of cloud computing from some IT department chiefs and the finance director may find himself as some sort of cloud arbiter.

The stakes are high for businesses. It will be a rare company that relies entirely on in-house IT in future. Some companies will move entirely to the cloud, some will move part of the infrastructure, some will move none. It's ▶

departments' real costs are assessed accurately there could be some resentment from those that have been undercharged in earlier years and now find their costs increasing (or resentment from departments that have been overcharged for several years). Either way, the finance director is likely to act as the diplomat smoothing over territorial disputes, ensuring the winners don't get triumphant and the losers don't become embittered.

Another key area the finance director must keep tabs on is licensing. Many

The stakes are high for businesses. It will be a rare company that relies entirely on in-house IT in future

a decision that's going to require some careful assessment of the pros and cons and the finance director will play a vital role in assessing the financial rationale.

For the IT director

IT directors have a different path to cloud. They have been aware of the debate and some of the buzzwords: public cloud; private cloud; software-as-a-service; outsourcing; cloud-sourcing; crowd-sourcing. But, unusually, these terms are just as likely to have come from the board as from the IT side.

For once, the majority of hardcore techies and their sources have underplayed the significance of cloud. This is partly because it's perceived as a threat – outsource services and you'll surely lose part of your team, is the thinking – but also because for them it's an emergent set of trends in virtualisation and hosting: a confection, made out of pre-existing components with the key innovations happening several years ago.

This makes the balance of emails hitting inboxes of IT directors all the stranger; a vast number of people, with salespeople in the vanguard, are attaching the word cloud to their sales pitches as if it's their road to personal salvation. In this new world the cloud is the outsourcing industry's wholehearted attack on the massive budgets and imposing empires of corporate IT. That's why less tech-savvy board colleagues love it so much. It isn't easy for an IT director to reject all these overtures.

Among the ambitious Powerpoint presentations there'll be a quiet voice from a clever guy who promises to chop your re-investment costs by 75%, without moving a corporate dataset outside your building. That last guy is

talking about private clouds, which is the data centre, virtualised and shrunk, and made mobile (in the sense that it can move from one compute host to another, and nothing at all to do with the iPhone).

IT directors who get drawn into an early-adopter, single-purpose cloud-badged project, could find themselves in great difficulty if they don't check details carefully. This is because the momentum of the optimistic, ignorant and misguided can be an astonishing thing, and because the hosting business has very little in the way of verification, standards, agreed procedures, or compensation packages for the day when something goes rather amiss. Hosting underpins cloud, and also wage packets if the IT director bets the company's operations on it.

Cloud companies that don't present rational means of running their services when their own platforms are offline are scarcely credible to seasoned technologists – so you have to be able to say, "What happens when it does not work?"

The answer lies with a private cloud. If sales teams are expected to do thousands of deals a day on an externally hosted service, then replicating that data internally on a compatible virtualisation platform is an insurance policy against not just kit failure at the software-as-a-service provider but also the sudden loss of your own Internet connection, perhaps traced to a telco's engineering works in the street outside.

In all likelihood, the eventual impact of cloud concepts will be somewhat less than the hopeful CEO – dreaming of losing his entire IT department – currently thinks. But it will also be a lot greater than the scornful nerd, looking at the toolbox cloud uses for delivery and finding nothing new or clever about it, is currently able to foresee.

It's also possible for an IT director to be in a business so secure, or so closely tied to physical processes, or so hugely dependent on a specific and ancient software suite, that there's no chance of making use of the high-profile parts of cloud computing. Companies running a factory floor of milling machines, or a metro line full of ticket readers, will find it difficult to run an on-demand capacity expansion project.

What the IT director does find difficult is to show that cloud computing has been assessed as a possibility. There'll be a lot of pressure on them from less 'techie' board members and it's important that the cloud option has been thoroughly investigated.

For the chief executive

The modern CEO isn't going to be short of advice in his attempt to get up-to-speed with cloud computing. But many of the opinions will be proffered by a host of vendors, cloud providers and channel partners – all of which will have their own agenda.

So, where does the CEO look to get the best advice on a move to the cloud? There are some things to focus on at the highest level, which lower-level managers and 'direct reports' won't necessarily have at the forefront of their minds. Terminology is one of those things. Your irritation at technical types babbling away using terms they don't define, no matter how well-intended you can see they are, gets some real teeth when it comes to cloud topics. There are a multitude of definitions out there, so how do you sort out which is best?

The top priority for any CEO contemplating a move to the cloud is to check the small print as if your life depends on it – because it could be that your business will come to depend on it. If you're unsure, consult with lawyers.

Cloud is about delivery of services and ensuring that cloud providers meet with their responsibilities. Research from Queen Mary College in 2010 revealed a wide disparity of wording within cloud computing contracts. This is one area where the small print is not to be ignored as the contract will be the basis for the way that the company runs – indeed it could be crucial to whether the company survives or not if things don't go quite to plan.

What happens when a cloud provider ▶

> **Cloud companies that don't present rational means of running services when their own platforms are offline are scarcely credible to technologists**

Enterprise cloud means business agility

PricewaterhouseCoopers (PwC) recommends the following:

1. Start by knowing where the organisation stands on the cloud computing continuum. Use benchmarking and gap analysis to understand where you are today
2. Conceptualise and communicate a compelling vision for using cloud computing to advance business objectives
3. Develop a cloud strategy and execution plan that incorporates any ad hoc components implemented already and lays out a systematic approach to moving forward
4. Understand the goal, which is not to get to cloud computing, but to achieve ever-greater levels of business efficiency and agility
5. Progress systematically through the five levels* of cloud computing components, realising that not all components are appropriate in all situations
6. Balance the use of private and public clouds to form a hybrid cloud that draws on both private and public cloud resources as needed
7. Focus on automation, which is the key to efficiency, agility and scalability

* SET OUT IN PWC'S PAPER, 'CLOUDS IN THE ENTERPRISE: NAVIGATING THE PATH TO BUSINESS ADVANTAGE', AVAILABLE AT WWW.PWC.COM

is hit by a denial-of-service attack? What stops a provider from moving data to another jurisdiction for cost or legal reasons? Is the provider the definitive provider-of-last-resort, or is it just reselling someone else's package? What happens if a customer wants to move providers or go back to in-premise? Due diligence isn't just a tick box in taking up services in the cloud, it's a major component of the project time.

The next question for an organisation to consider is how closely it wants to work with its cloud provider. Some will be hands-off and see themselves as a facility for handling peak demands. Some will be more personal and try to be intimately involved in their customers' business. Be wary though: the dream of many of the upsellers in the current wave of cloud hype is to pretend to be removable, when in fact they fully intend to hook customers for the foreseeable future. Keeping independence is very much a CEO-level question, as is the exit strategy. Cloud is meant to be all about steering work to an available resource, not watching it vanish behind someone else's security gates.

Cloud computing presents the CEO with a major opportunity to reshape and reorganise their business. It's not just about IT, it's about how to use, analyse and improve company data and it's about using IT to have an impact on business processes. Many companies have operated on the 'we've always done things this way' principle – cloud computing will offer the opportunity to do away with this thinking.

Cloud computing may not be for every business or every CEO but every one should be looking at the technology. The best companies will be those where the board looks at the direction the organisation is headed over the next five years and the best means for getting there. If that involves cloud, now is the best time to be thinking about it. If not, your competitors will be. ■

Better hosting

For the last five years PC Pro readers
have voted us "Best Web Host".

Isn't it time you found out why?

Cloud and SMEs# Cloud and small firms – a great match

Small organisations are obvious candidates for cloud computing – but there's still an awareness issue and SMEs should tread carefully, says **Maxwell Cooter**

CLOUD COMPUTING IS an unusual phenomenon in the IT world as it is being used equally by small businesses and enterprises. Indeed, it's the smaller businesses that should benefit most as they are the companies that tend not to have large IT departments. Some small companies have no IT departments at all and are serviced by someone doing the job in his spare time, or by a local services company.

This is not the norm when it comes to technology. The natural order of things is for IT advances to start off in large businesses and work their way downwards: mobile phones started as an executive toy, now everyone has one; routers were part of the arcane global telecoms world, now people are connected at home.

Cloud computing has been different – there are many instances of SMEs adopting cloud-based delivery wholeheartedly, while larger enterprises have hesitated. Indeed, Andy Burton of the UK's Cloud Industry Forum believes that cloud computing is the first case of a technology that started in small businesses and has moved to larger ones.

Is the UK lagging behind?

But that's not the complete picture. In reality things are not entirely rosy for the cloud and SMEs. There have been some very enterprising small businesses who have been happy to adopt cloud as the backbone of their IT set-up but there's also a good deal of scepticism.

A survey in 2011 revealed some of this hesitancy. According to VMware, a provider of virtualisation software, only 48% of British SMEs had begun using cloud technology. While this looks encouraging, the same survey found that 60% of small businesses across Europe were going down this path. Other surveys have found even larger gaps in adoption and one reported that 43% of SME respondents didn't even know what the term meant.

There are two problems with this: for a start, there are millions of people who are happily using consumer cloud services, such as Facebook and Google Mail, not to mention commercial cloud applications such as Google Apps and various smartphone apps. Second, figures from analyst IDC have shown that small businesses do not appear to be miserly when it comes to cloud – £9.8 billion was spent on cloud technologies in 2009 and half the figure came from SME budgets, it reports.

The seeming gap between the perception of cloud and expenditure can almost certainly be explained by a lack of understanding of what cloud is. There's a

38   The Ultimate Guide to Cloud Computing   cloudpro.co.uk

Cloud computing is thought to be the first case of a technology that started in small businesses and has moved to larger ones

good chance that business people are using cloud services – even if they don't actually know it.

Software: the choice is yours

The other issue is that small companies tend not to be burdened with large legacy systems or have equipment that need to integrated in a cloud service. That's not to say that some do not have bespoke applications and specialist computer kit that may take time to phase out.

But if you're operating a start-up, there is little need to run any sort of IT facilities at all. By opting for Google Apps or Microsoft's new Office 365 cloud suite, a business could have all its productivity software (word processing, calendar, email and so on) working in the cloud. The business could also use accountancy software such as KashFlow to run its financials, Salesforce.com to handle its customer relationships and any number of software packages to look after its HR, marketing and procurement.

Higher up the scale, NetSuite offers cloud ERP (enterprise resource planning) software – the type of package that's normally the preserve of large businesses. In fact, just about every aspect of a modern day business could be run on cloud-based software.

And it's not just new cloud vendors that are providing options for these ▶

companies: plenty of long-established software firms are now in on the act. Accountancy software specialist, Sage, has released its own cloud-based software, ERP specialist SAP has taken its first steps down the cloud route and Oracle is embracing the technology, despite CEO Larry Ellison's initially dismissive remarks about cloud.

The most remarkable transformation of all has been Microsoft, which is a mainstay for so many small organisations in all sectors of the economy. The company's reputation has been built on boxed products and its licensing methodology had been geared towards this. But in 2010, Microsoft's CEO, Steve Ballmer, said that the company was betting its future on the cloud and since then it has looked to turn that vision into reality.

Office 365 is its step in that direction although Microsoft, unlike Google, its rival in the productivity suite stakes, has

not quite managed to divorce itself from its roots and Office 365 does require some access to elements such as Exchange, SharePoint and Lync. Google does offer a 100% cloud-based, standalone product with Google Apps, which many companies are turning to – although the company did lose some popularity when it reduced the number of users supported in its free version from 50 to 10.

A picture of what smaller companies are adopting when it comes to the cloud comes from US industry association CompTIA, which in a 2011 survey reports that storage and backup solutions are the most heavily used cloud applications (71% of SMEs using the cloud), followed by email (62%), document management (59%), collaboration (56%) and customer relationship management (53%).

Microsoft's CEO, Steve Ballmer, said that the company was betting its future on the cloud

About a third of SMEs, it adds, are using cloud services, and an overwhelming majority – 92% – say their experience has been positive or very positive.

Counting on cost savings

But it's not just the availability of heaps of software that's attractive to small business. There are also financial benefits. One of the biggest problems facing start-ups is cashflow, and the onset of cloud has reduced the cost of getting off the ground significantly in the last decade. The arrival of cloud has also made it easier to plan – financial forecasting becomes easier – and paying for services is now more simple. There are no more visits to the bank manager trying to argue about credit arrangements: a whole IT infrastructure can be arranged by the judicious use

Key issues for small businesses

- Start small and build up – don't overprovision
- The pay-as-you-go ethos is helpful but keep an eye on costs, PAYG can work out more expensive than on-premise; be sensible in your planning
- Have a proper back-up and disaster recovery process in place – if something can go wrong, it will
- Make sure that you're buying services from a reputable supplier – there is a lot of 'cloud washing' (ie. deceptive marketing) out there
- You're still responsible for compliance – don't pass the buck to your provider when it comes to conforming to regulations

of the company credit card.

But not only that, there's no longer a need to guess what computer resources are needed: a company owner can now afford to start small and build up after the revenue has come in.

Having made the decision to go with cloud, the next stage is to work out the hardware: if you're not going to run with a server under your desk or tucked away in a corner somewhere, you're going to need a cloud service provider. Again, there are a host of providers to choose from, ranging from those who will provide you with your own remote server or a virtual server (that is, one dedicated to you or shared with other companies in a public cloud).

The company that really kick-started the cloud ethos for small organisations is Amazon. The company realised that it had a large amount of under-used IT resources and it started selling some of its spare computing and storage capacity. Amazon Web Services now has a massive share of the market – in August 2011, the company announced that its cloud division was now a billion dollar business in its own right. It offers a range of cloud products but its main ones are EC2 (Elastic Compute Cloud) and S3 (Simple Storage Service), both of which are widely used by small businesses around the world.

Beware the small print

However, while it sounds like it could be a perfect match, there are still issues for SMEs to consider. Regardless of the size of the contract, it's still essential to get a contract checked to ensure that it covers all possibilities.

Companies would have more piece of mind if vendors had some form of certification: the UK's Cloud Industry Forum offers a self-certified code of practice that several companies (including Microsoft) have signed up to. Alternatively, there's a more rigorous offering in the pipeline under the banner of another industry organisation, Eurocloud. This accreditation scheme, the Eurocloud Star Assessment, is not self-certified and costs the vendor a lot more to attain.

After checking the provenance of a cloud supplier, the details of its contract, formulating a disaster recovery plan and provisioning the initial services, then a company is ready to go. Many SMEs will have used a reseller to handle this part of the business, in which case it's important to know what after-sales plans are in place. Many resellers have been suspicious of cloud but the good ones know that it presents a new opportunity and are ready to meet the challenge – a helpful reseller will be invaluable in this process.

Small businesses and cloud computing make a natural fit – even if they don't always realise it. There may be some hesitancy out there but we're going to see most small organisations turn to the cloud in the future. ∎

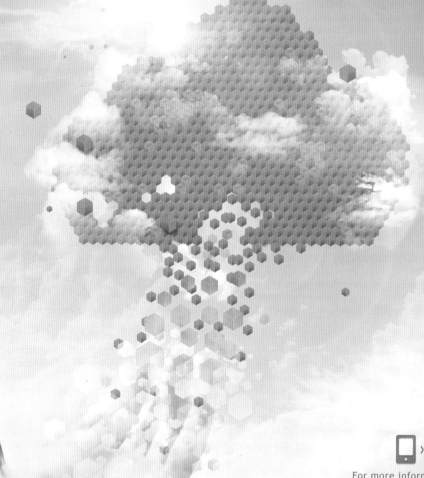

The power of Cloud Computing
at your fingertips

What to look out for in
CLOUD CONTRACTS

If you rely on a public cloud service you could be in for a shock if the service goes down, as **Lesley Meall** describes

IT'S ALL VERY WELL being charged only for the computing power you use – as long as it is there when you want it. So the outage of Amazon's Elastic Cloud Compute (EC2) service in April 2011 – when some users were offline for several days, an eternity in today's trading world – made a lot of people understandably very unhappy. It brought a wry smile to the faces of observers who said it was only a matter of time before something like this happened, although not because cloud computing is inherently risky.

The incredulous cries of unhappy Amazon users showed just how little attention many had paid to the small print before they signed up. As Martyn Hart, chairman of the National Outsourcing Association (NOA), says: "Cloud computing is not like normal outsourcing," meaning that contracts can be far less rigorous than when signing up with say a payroll supplier. That said, private cloud contracts, at least, can look a lot like traditional managed services, which in turn can be much like outsourcing as we know it.

But public cloud services, which many smaller organisations are now using for vital parts of their business such as email ▶

and payments, can leave a lot to be desired when it comes to service level agreements (SLAs), which are one of the mainstays in outsourcing and services contracts.

"Some providers of public cloud services don't offer a formal SLA," observes Craig West, a sales director at NetSuite, one of the leading business software players with cloud offerings. This is particularly so in the 'one contract size fits all' world of software-as-a-service. "I think that we may be unique among software providers in offering an SLA with an uptime guarantee," he suggests, adding that if his company doesn't maintain its promised 99.5% uptime in any given month, then customers will have their monthly subscription returned.

West freely admits that the form this takes is a credit to your account (and if you've lost money because of system downtime, this will be small recompense), but this particular remedy tends to be the norm among software-as-a-service providers. "The balance of power sits with the service provider," observes Hart, and you don't have to wade very far into most public cloud providers' carefully worded 'terms of service' to see how little they resemble a formal SLA.

This lack of formality is present in most public cloud services, and it's something that looms large on the radar of any specialist solicitor (or experienced buyer of managed services). "Some organisations really understand the nature of what they're entering into," reports Ian Marriott, at analyst Gartner. "If they have been involved in lots of

these types of relationship there is a level of knowledge and expertise that enables them to appreciate the challenge."

The trouble is that cloud computing has put the power to select, commission and pay for IT services into the hands of people who do not always appreciate the need for thorough (and ongoing) due diligence. According to Gartner, it is essential that those planning to contract for cloud services do a "deep analysis on the impact and probability of the risks", mitigate for the issues that they consider most critical, and then revisit them at frequent intervals during the lifetime of the contract – though understanding these risks calls for more than a passing acquaintance with contract law.

So, what can buyers of cloud services do to protect themselves? Well that depends on who you ask, which type of cloud service you are using or planning to use, and the size and type of organisation that is both buying them

> **Cloud computing has put the power to select IT into the hands of people who do not always appreciate the need for due diligence**

Contracts summary

Here's a quick checklist when it comes to contracts:

- Evaluate how much you're willing to pay to ensure your move to the cloud doesn't end up losing you money, or your business
- Review the level of service from the provider. Does it provide adequate protection?
- Take appropriate steps – through your provider or otherwise – to ensure you have a disaster recovery plan that works
- Consider what the provider is liable for and what has been excluded. Is this an acceptable level of risk?

and providing them. At a recent conference on cloud computing, lawyer Marc Lindsey, a partner with the Washington DC law firm LB3, firmly advised enterprises to protect themselves by "demanding" that cloud service providers "put their own money at risk" and offer "liquid damages for SLA violations".

In practice, this is only possible if the relationship between the service provider and the buyer is an equitable one, where the balance of power and the balance of risk are not so clearly one-sided – as is the case with most public cloud service providers and smaller firms that is typical of their customer bases. An SME user of a public cloud service that is unhappy with what's being provided (or not provided) has little ammunition.

With little negotiating power, they appear to have a choice between voting with their feet or following Gartner's

recommendations. But the latter means expending time, money and other resources on a risk analysis, and then devoting more time, money and resources to building resilience into their own systems, or factoring the cost of not doing so into the cloud computing cost-benefit analysis they should have done, but probably didn't. All of which makes public clouds seem a lot less appealing.

Then again, maybe there's another option. Despite his disinclination to consider cloud computing as outsourcing, Hart at the NOA has some advice on contracts and relationships that could stand future SME buyers of public cloud services in good stead. "Think about the balance of power when you choose your supplier," he suggests, and try to match the size of their business to the size of your business. "You don't want to be a small fish in a giant pond." ∎

ONCE YOU'VE MADE the decision to move away from computer systems that are physically located within your organisation, there's another problem to solve, and that's the contract you need to have with a provider.

The type of contract that you have with the cloud provider (or a reseller of the cloud provider's service) is crucial. Get this part wrong and your business could be looking at some serious financial consequences.

There are three main areas to concentrate on: reliability, security and liability, and you should be paying keen attention to a cloud provider's policy on all of them.

Is it reliable?

Reliability is about the technical performance of the cloud provider's service. Do their servers go down? What mirroring options do they have in place? What monitoring systems do they have in place? You should be prepared to carry out due diligence on the cloud companies and assess their performance. Look at the company's past performance – does it have a good reputation?

On the other hand, cloud companies may point out that having an IT infrastructure in-house does not necessarily mean that your servers or network are more reliable. They will say that managing data centres is their core business and will claim that they're much better at managing this infrastructure than user organisations.

However, while it's true that cloud providers will tend to have more robust and better managed infrastructures, you need more reassurance than that. It's vital that all the fine details are built into the service. And the type of cloud provider is important here – one factor to bear in mind is that buying a standard package from a larger operator will leave very little room to manoeuvre, while customising an offering from a smaller reseller could offer a more flexible experience.

CONTRACTS
what to focus on

Frank Jennings, a senior partner at DMH Stallard, gives an overview of the main areas to look at when entering into a cloud computing deal

Be secure

There are a couple of factors to consider when it comes to security. If you are in financial services you have to conform with the Financial Services Act and all companies will have to consider the Data Protection Act and the scrutiny of the Information Commissioner. And offending organisations can be hit by big fines: the FSA fined HSBC £3m for losing data, for example.

To be blunt, the liability for any breaches of security or privacy lies with you – so you need to be concerned with the consequences of handing over information to a third party. It's very important to ensure that cloud providers are taking proper steps to protect data. Are they keeping it in the EU, as they're legally obliged to do, rather than sending it over to India? Some insist that UK data is housed in the UK – that's not legally necessary but it does give added peace of mind.

Although you as the customer are ultimately liable, there are steps that can be taken. You must include in the contract where the data is held and who it can be released to. There should also be an indemnity clause that stipulates that the cloud provider has taken all possible precautions to avoid security breaches and takes legal responsibility for any losses.

Ultimately, however, market forces will come into play. If a company loses data, then its reputation will suffer – cloud companies are going to stand or fall by their reliability and a few security breaches will quickly destroy that.

> **Liability for any breaches of security lies with you. Be concerned about the consequences of handing data to a third party**

Who is liable?

The third factor to look at is liability – what happens when things go wrong with the day to day service? Again, levels of compensation need to be placed in the contract but money will be of little satisfaction to a customer that has gone bust.

Some cloud providers try to exclude liability, rather in the same way that insurance companies will look not to pay out on their policies – although you could get around this by taking out your own insurance.

Another option is that cloud providers will offer some sort of protection but this will involve paying a higher fee for a gold or platinum service. This could mean that the cloud company is offering a more robust service, say at a high quality data centre with better monitoring facilities. Or it could be ▶

IN DEPTH: top nine contract areas to watch

Analyst firm Gartner suggests the following contract issues to consider when signing up with a cloud computing provider:

1 **Uptime guarantees** – Gartner says it has seen many contracts that have no uptime or performance service-level guarantees

2 **Service-level agreement (SLA) penalties** – these should be financial and ideally money-back and not credits

3 **SLA penalty exclusion** – look carefully at exclusions to penalties, such as ensuring a downtime calculation starts exactly when the downtime starts

4 **Security** – Gartner says the provider's security practices should be at the same level as, or exceed, your own practices, especially for national privacy-related regulations. It recommends negotiating SLAs for security breaches

5 **Business continuity and disaster recovery** – contracts rarely contain any provisions for disaster recovery, says Gartner, and some providers take no action to back-up

customer data. You should ensure there is access to your own back-up measures where necessary

6 **Data privacy conditions** – no personal data sharing should take place but contracts can be complex where there are multiple suppliers (eg. both a software and platform provider is used)

7 **Suspension of service** – best to have an agreement that payments in any current legitimate dispute should not lead to a suspension of service, says Gartner

8 **Termination** – provider contracts often have 30 day termination clauses – look to extend this where possible

9 **Liability** – Gartner recommends aiming for better liability protection than just a return of yearly fees.

SOURCE: IT PROCUREMENT BEST PRACTICE: NINE CONTRACTUAL TERMS TO REDUCE RISK IN CLOUD CONTRACTS – GARTNER

based on the fact that the cloud company is prepared to pay more if things go wrong.

Bear in mind too that you may sign up not with the cloud service provider but with a reseller, which could introduce another level of complication. You will be signing on the reseller's terms but there could well be a clash with the cloud hosting company – the cloud company could be providing a bronze level of service while the reseller could be offering a gold one.

One way round this is

by signing a pass-through contract where the reseller supplies a service from a named supplier such as Amazon or Microsoft.

There's no doubt that the market will consolidate over the next few years as the poorer providers are found out and smaller cloud companies will be taken over. While that's happening, look to sign up with an accredited cloud provider, a company that has been endorsed by the Cloud Industry Forum or ISO, for example.

But one thing is certain: the due diligence work needs to be carried out up-front – there is little opportunity for comeback after a problem, whether it's a security breach or a service issue. ■

> **Due diligence work needs to be carried out up-front – there is little opportunity for comeback after a problem**

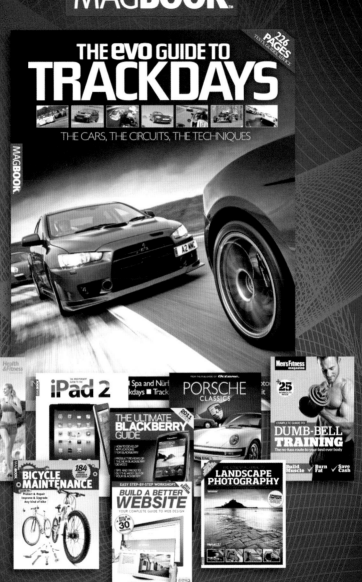

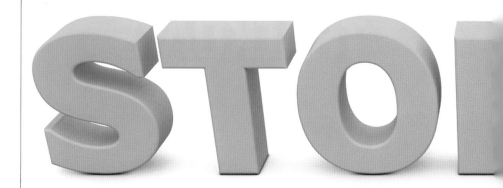

DATA STORAGE IN THE CLOUD
– now any firm can benefit

Offsite data backup has long been a staple of enterprise disaster recovery strategy but has been too expensive or complex for smaller organisations. That's all changed now, as **Davey Winder** explains

The benefits are significant...

It doesn't take a genius to work out that multiple copies of your data, stored across disparate servers, is much safer than having all your data eggs in one basket. But that can cost a lot of money if it's your own hardware, so look to the cloud where a service provider will be able to duplicate your data across multiple, geographically distributed servers. Not only does this significantly cut the chances of all your data being lost, it also brings the same disaster recovery strategies used by large enterprises within reach of much smaller companies.

Complexity costs money, both in terms of infrastructure (such as tape drives, virtual machines, offsite storage and technical staff to maintain it all) and also business downtime (if you have data on tape drives at offsite storage and need to restore servers, the time to recovery becomes stretched). Keeping it simple in the cloud allows smaller organisations to budget for business continuity, with the added value of virtually instant data recovery.

...but watch out for pitfalls

The biggest pitfall of a cloud-based disaster recovery strategy is that you may be at risk with a single supplier. While the ability of the cloud to provide data redundancy across multiple and disparate servers gives a huge amount of confidence, you also have to allow for the worse case scenario: your cloud provider going out of business and taking timely access to your data with it. So to guarantee business continuity, retaining a full backup on your own servers or contracting a secondary cloud service might be wise.

Service level agreements (SLAs) are a vital part of any cloud contract, but they are not a magic bullet that can save your business if things go pear shaped at your cloud storage provider. No matter how contractually watertight your SLA is, if things go wrong all it actually provides is legal leverage. Ensure, therefore, that your SLA explicitly details an agreed remediation process in event of failure so that your business does not suffer unduly while waiting for compensation to arrive.

Get the priorities right

Asking the right questions of a cloud storage provider is essential if both the transition to a cloud-based disaster recovery process and its effectiveness once in place are to be trouble free. Proper investigation is vital when it comes to determining if a provider can meet the needs of your business in terms ▶

> **If a cloud provider falls at any of the other due diligence hurdles then it is unsuitable to be trusted with your data**

of compliance, security, data handling and recovery.

In fact, the specifics of the data recovery aspects of the service are probably the last things that you should investigate and for good reason: if a cloud provider falls at any of the other due diligence hurdles then it is unsuitable to be trusted with your data.

Remember that cloud-based storage services are still relatively immature, and with companies keen to jump on the bandwagon before the wheels start wobbling it is vital to ensure that any service provider you contract with has an established track record. You will want to know how long they have been trading and how financially stable they are.

It's not that start-up companies are definitely off the radar, but be sure to take into account the impact on your data should a small company be bought out by a larger one that you may have already discounted for whatever reason. So be sure to properly investigate how easy it is to move your data to another provider should you want to terminate your contract at any point.

Security and compliance
If your industry is covered by specific regulatory requirements then your next question must be whether the provider can adhere to them. Obviously, if it

cannot, or is unsure, then it's not worth asking any more questions. If it can, then move on to matters of security. Ask obvious question such as how your data is encrypted, and less obvious ones such as who holds the encryption keys.

Ask about who has access to your data and what controls are in place to prevent both accidental and intentional abuse, but also ask about physical security at the data centres. If your service provider is unable or unwilling to answer your security questions, find one that is.

CLOUD STORAGE – benefits summary

Cloud storage can address many challenges that physical storage doesn't:

- You are not dependent on a single server
- There is no direct dependency on any hardware
- You don't have to buy more disk space than you initially need to accommodate future data growth
- Business continuity is provided in the event of a site disaster
- A 'virtual' storage container can be provisioned that is larger than the physical space available
- You can drastically reduce over-provisioning in a pay-as-you-go model
- You can access your entire storage pool from a single point.

SOURCE: WWW.I365.COM

What about the worse case scenario?

We've already mentioned SLAs, but even though an agreement will not save your data if everything goes wrong, a properly negotiated one could save your business. Ask about business critical issues such as availability, security and compensation from the start. Deal only with a service provider that is willing to enter into detailed negotiations about the SLA.

To mitigate any need to resort to the SLA, be sure also to ask the provider for full details of its own data protection, recovery and auditing procedures, and don't be afraid to prod them all with your due diligence stick.

What, where and how many?

This is data storage and disaster recovery we are talking about, so be sure to ask appropriate questions of any provider such as how many copies of your data sets are kept, where they are located geographically and how far back your archive stretches. Don't be afraid to get technical and ask about the frequency of data verification tests and availability of verification reports. ■

Crunching the numbers

Would you weigh up the financial benefits of the cloud?
Or is it a 'no brainer'? **Lesley Meall** asks the right questions

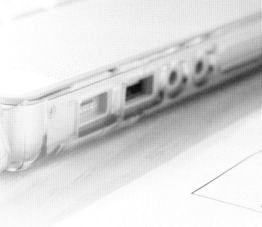

WE ARE ALL AWARE of the need to factor financial considerations into any technology-related decision-making process – but this doesn't make it easy to do. So although accounting concepts such as net present value (NPV), return on investment (ROI) and total cost of ownership (TCO) are routinely used to estimate and compare IT costs, as Chas Roy-Chowdhury, head of taxation at the Association of Chartered Certified Accountants points out, there is plenty of room for interpretation, and "you could have a situation where two accountants end up with different figures".

It's not hard to understand why. Whether you are considering using software-as-a-service (SaaS), or comparing alternatives such as public clouds and private clouds, or totting up the bill for maintaining the status quo, there are many cost-related factors to consider. These range from set-up, service and training, to overheads such as floor space and electricity, to less tangible costs such as those associated with security breaches and their impact on reputation.

Then there are the implications of cloud computing for tax and financial reporting, and the great CAPEX vs OPEX debate.

"It's difficult to work out the cost associated with any technology purchasing decision, but cloud computing is more challenging," says Roy-Chowdhury, citing barriers such as not being able to compare like with like. "You pay forever to use cloud services," he observes, which adds up to some pretty big TCO numbers. But as he adds: "Being able to access information and infrastructure any time and from anywhere is very advantageous, and the

short-term benefits of cloud computing may outweigh the long-term cost."

All of which helps to explain why some cost-related decisions on cloud computing seem to have more to do with gut feeling than hard numbers. "We didn't do any detailed analysis financially before deciding to run the business in the cloud," says Gary White, chief executive of White Springs, which is both a provider and user of cloud computing services. But even though the financial analysis was done only "at a high level" he says "the decision was a no-brainer, because the benefits of subscribing to Salesforce.com [the customer relationship management provider] versus buying and owning the hardware and software were absolutely clear", and the gains weren't just to do with cost.

Cross-company visibility

White Springs is a fast-growing UK company with operations in Europe and the US, so it was obvious to White that putting in his own infrastructure would require huge resources, and impede the development of the business. "I wanted my staff to focus on growing the firm, not on running the infrastructure," he says, White Springs did start with a PC accounts system, but as soon as FinancialForce.com (accounting that runs on Salesforce.com) was available, it switched. "Gaining greater functionality and visibility of customer and financial information across the company was more important than the long-term cost of doing it," he adds.

While the benefits of SaaS may be so great that the long-term financial costs seem like an irrelevance, things are less straightforward in the world of virtual data centres and infrastructure-as-a-service (IaaS), from the point of view of technology and finance. Cloud purists

may draw a line around public clouds (such as Amazon Web Services) and decry private clouds and hybrid clouds as oxymorons, but once these terms entered the marketing-speak of vendors such as Cisco and IBM, cloud computing was further redefined, so businesses may as well acknowledge this and consider the relative costs of all the available options.

The decision-making process is not necessarily a private data centre and an on-demand data centre (ie. IaaS). It's a more complex choice that also includes all sorts of hosted and managed services (many of which you will find described as types of cloud). It's not an 'all or nothing' choice either, because there is the possibility of combining on-demand public resources with those provided by your own data centre (whether that's software applications, computing power,

> **One of the big benefits of SaaS is its capacity to relieve the user of all of the burdens associated with software maintenance and upgrades**

Somebody has to be responsible for monitoring, managing and patching your on-demand infrastructure. There are software tools designed specifically to help you do all of this, and with minimal technical knowledge and no programming skills, but while some organisations are comfortable doing this themselves, others prefer to hand it over to a third party. That's one of the reasons why a variety of hosted, managed service and outsourced solutions are being labelled and marketed as private clouds, and one of the reasons why there are so many possible approaches to financing all of these different types of cloud.

For example, in a private cloud where you pay for the software licences and you own the computer servers, there are various ways to avoid taking the hit up front. Financing options include contract hire, hire purchase, loans and various types of lease.

A private cloud can't exploit the buying power of the public cloud, so the costs may be higher, and unless you invest in some very big servers, you aren't going to have the elasticity of the public cloud (though you may think you're never going to need it). But you can exploit virtualisation to better use the computing resources you do have in a private cloud.

No room for internal IT
Silverdell, an asbestos removal and management contractor, considered all these factors when it was contemplating the sorry state of its IT infrastructure. "After a series of acquisitions we had three operating divisions at 25 locations and a hotchpotch of systems," explains chief financial officer, Ian Johnson. "When we reviewed the IT infrastructure and support we quickly realised we weren't big enough to support our own internal IT team," he says, and after ▶

or file storage – which may or may not be managed in-house, or hosted – or outsourced, if you want to split hairs), in what's often described as a 'hybrid cloud' solution.

Ups and downs of IaaS
The decision on which to opt for may not be as much of a 'no brainer' as choosing SaaS over the on-premise alternative. Although IaaS can provide you with 'elastic' access to computing power, memory and storage, and is charged on a pay-as-you-go basis only for the resources used (without installing new equipment or waiting out the hardware procurement process), there is a downside. One of the big benefits of SaaS is its capacity to relieve the user of all of the burdens associated with software maintenance and upgrades; IaaS requires a little more attention.

Financial benefits of cloud computing and services

Factor	On-premise	Cloud computing
Expenditure type	Capital expenditure (capex) Operating expense (opex)	Operating expense (opex)
Cash flow	Servers and software are purchased upfront	Payments are made as the service is provided
Financial risk	Entire financial risk is taken upfront, with uncertain return	Financial risk is taken monthly and is matched to return
Income statement	Maintenance and depreciated capital expense	Maintenance expense only
Balance sheet	Software and hardware are carried as a long-term capital asset	Nothing appears on the balance sheet

SOURCE: TALKING TO YOUR CFO ABOUT CLOUD COMPUTING, FORRESTER RESEARCH

considering various options, Silverdell decided that a private cloud and virtual desktops were the most cost-effective solution.

Silverdell owns its own servers and pays for traditional software licences, but Johnson says: "For what one competent IT head would have cost us, we were able to get a hosted solution." This provides web-based access to processing power and applications, and the desktops have been virtualised for the three Silverdell operating divisions – also using the most cost-effective solution.

"We considered Citrix and Microsoft desktop virtualisation, but 2X [another virtual desktop player] offered the best price-performance ratio," says John Abrahams, technical director with IT Managed Services, which manages Silverdell's software licences, infrastructure maintenance and staff

support, in an arrangement that is backed up by a custom service level agreement (SLA).

These are rare among providers of public cloud services, but if you don't factor the terms of your SLA into your cost-benefit analyses, you could end up paying for services you can't use, or have no intention of using.

Which is what happened to one software engineer who didn't read his Amazon Web Services contract well enough to know what he would be billed for; when the meter would be running; and when it would stop. "I put some test virtual machines on the servers of AWS, and for a while my bills were just a few pennies each, so when I got a monthly bill for $40 I was a bit surprised," says Adam Ramsay. "Turns out, when I finished the tests, I forgot to turn off the network." ■

It's been hard to enough making sense of traditional software licenses – now the cloud means things may get more complicated, warns **Lesley Meall**

SOFTWARE LICENCES
- a state of flux

FREEDOM OF CHOICE can sometimes feel like a mixed blessing. Take the recently released Microsoft Office 365, the software giant's new cloud service that combines its productivity offerings such as Word and Powerpoint. On the one hand, you can now choose from numerous variants of Microsoft-hosted Offices (P1, K1, K2, E1, E2, E3, E4, and so on), and you can use them instead of, or mixed with, other approaches to providing remote and local access to MS Office tools; on the other hand, you could

lose the will to live trying to work out how to license all of this or estimate how much it is eventually going to cost you.

In the time-honoured tradition of the software industry, licensing for Microsoft Office can be rather opaque, particularly for enterprise users. You may be able to figure out which variant you would need if you were radical enough to want to access Office 365 from somewhere such as an airport kiosk or an Internet café (not all subscriptions allow this). But if you already have a traditional Office

▶

deployment, and you want to understand the differences between licensing Office as a 'software product' and as a 'subscription service' you face a challenge of a different order.

According to Microsoft, "the volume licensing of software makes it easier and more affordable to run software on multiple computers within a single purchasing organisation". Yes, well. The enterprise volume licensing arrangements for MS Office Professional

> **Working through software licensing issues requires a lot of upfront planning and moving to the cloud doesn't necessarily make this easier**

Plus for Office 365 are so complex that explaining them requires a seven page document, which is not an easy read.

This level of complexity is not unique to Microsoft. "Working through software licensing issues requires a lot of upfront planning," warns Amy Konary, an analyst at IDC, "and moving to the cloud doesn't necessarily make this easier." Licences for subscription-based public cloud services are relatively uncomplicated, but when organisations are trying to migrate some or all of their applications or infrastructure into hybrid or private clouds (hosted by the enterprise or by third parties), licensing is more complex.

"Negotiating with software vendors that have varying degrees of interest in cooperating with you can be excruciating," says Konary, and not just because you may have to go through the negotiation process on multiple occasions. "Attitudes may depend on your company's monetary and strategic value," she suggests, though in some

cases, the vendor won't have given their position this much thought. Konary's research indicates that many are currently deciding their policies 'on the fly', and that very few have yet to come up with 'cloud-friendly licensing'.

Software vendor CCH, an accounting specialist, is not untypical in being in a state of flux. "In the US we are moving very strongly towards on-demand cloud-based offerings," says Simon Crompton, executive director of CCH UK. But in the UK, some of its software products are available only via traditional on-premise installations, despite being available as both on-premise and on-demand offerings in the US. "We are very open minded and pragmatic about the cloud," he adds. "If clients ask for something we look at it and consider the commercial implications.'"

So what happens if a UK client wants to build their own private cloud and virtualise some CCH applications? Well, the software licensing is based on the traditional 'concurrent users' model and the minimum contract term remains one year, which isn't very flexible. "We have used temporary licences to support clients during peak processing periods in the past," recalls Crompton, but he's talking about years ago, when a change in legislation created some one-time 'seasonal spikes' that affected lots of CCH users. At the moment, he says: "There isn't a demand for this."

Hybrid licensing

Meanwhile Unit4, a business software player, has gone further, as Ton Dobbe, vice president of product management explains. "We have put in place integration between Agresso Business World and FinancialForce.com," he says, adding that these are both owned by Unit4, and provide customers with mixed access to on-premise and on-demand versions of products. "We already have some organisations doing this with Agresso," says Dobbe, where most of the system is licensed and accessed in the traditional manner, but applications such as expenses and payroll are licensed on a subscription basis.

Unit 4 also supports other approaches to software licensing and subscription. "This reflects the needs of the public and private sector, vertical markets, and different countries," says Dobbe. So pricing may be based on the number of citizens in a city, active users, or levels of functionality. Facilities have also been built into Agresso so that users can see what their 'active consumption' of software licences is, whether they have an on-premise installation and are mixing this with on-demand (hosted by Unit4), or have their own private cloud (hosted internally or externally).

Benefits of a 'true-up' model

But in general, licence management is one of the biggest challenges of creating hybrid or private clouds. "In the absence of cloud-ready software licensing models, a negotiated approach with a true-up model is generally preferred," reports Konary, with IT departments opting for an annual true-up approach over quarterly or monthly comparisons – though more automation may change this. (A 'true-up' model is moving up to a usage band with, say, a higher set fee if you are consistently going over a limit and incurring extra costs.)

"Tools that help monitor licence use to make the true-up process less onerous are desired," she adds, as is a more cloud-friendly approach from many vendors. Meanwhile, freedom of choice can sometimes feel like a bit of a mixed blessing. ∎

Software licensing fact find

Few organisations know what software they are using

The vast majority of organisations have only partial knowledge of the software that they have deployed. A significant proportion have no monitoring tools in place capable of auditing what software is deployed, and even fewer have accurate information on what is actively in use. The result is significant operational risk and overspend.

The proliferation of licensing mechanisms is aggravating the problem

User, server, processor, site, enterprise and a number of other commercial licensing schemes are in common use, with organisations large and small often managing a complex mix of arrangements. Open source licences may or may not be used under subscription/support contracts.

Use of software-as-a-service (SaaS) is rising, but beware contract inflexibility

While 'utility' SaaS offerings such as hosted email are used the most, there is evidence of SaaS starting to be adopted for both core and departmental application needs. While this delivery option is still in the early stages of market acceptance, it looks set to take its place in the mainstream. Many, however, report that SaaS is not always as flexible as providers would have us believe.

Many licences and subscriptions are based on the 'ratchet' principle of commitment

On site or in the cloud, most commercial software arrangements appear to scale only one way – up. Reducing commitment is too often costly, difficult or even impossible. This artificial restriction on flexibility is perceived to exist to the benefit of suppliers, and potentially stands in the way of dynamic cloud based models being used to deal with fluctuating demands.

SOURCE: SOFTWARE LICENSING AND SUBSCRIPTION, FREEFORM DYNAMICS.
WWW.FREEFORMDYNAMICS.COM

The Cloud.
Distilled.

Everything you need to know about how cloud computing will change your business

www.cloudpro.co.uk

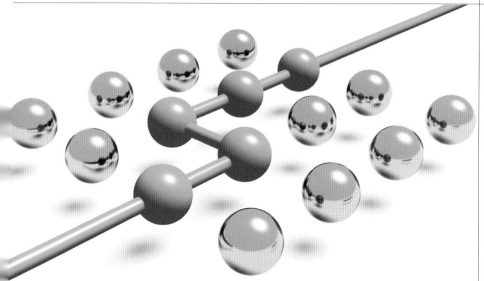

Is the cloud green?

Is cloud computing a greener way to go with IT? Yes, says
Maxwell Cooter, but it's a complex calculation to prove it in detail

SOMETHING STRANGE HAS happened in the last decade: green issues – which used to be the preserve of hippies and environmentalists – have quietly invaded the mainstream. One can scarcely look at a new service for anything these days without being reminded of its green credentials. New car? Fewer emissions. New boiler? Energy efficient. New lightbulb? Eco-friendly.

Needless to say, this philosophy has permeated the IT industry too with much more attention being paid to the energy rating of servers and PCs than there has been in previous years.

Cloud computing has been a key part of this debate and there's a long-running discussion on whether the technology is energy efficient or not. So how does a company interested in maintaining its green credentials go about deciding whether to go the cloud route or not? After all, you may need to show what your IT is consuming as part of a statutory carbon audit, especially in larger companies. Regulation on energy use can only increase in the future.

It's not an easy question to answer. On one hand, we have a school of thought that says because cloud computing data centres are not adding to the actual computing power, but are using servers more efficiently, then they are, by definition, the greener option. There are opponents, however, who say that there are some big questions to be answered first and that the blanket statement that cloud computing is greener is a misleading one. It's getting to be a heated debate – with both sides brandishing the figures to support their case.

The latest entrant in this form of climate war is research company, Verdantix, which released a report in 2011 claiming that American companies could drastically cut CO_2 emissions by turning to cloud computing. According to the report, a wholesale move to cloud delivery would deliver CO_2 emission reductions of 85.7m tonnes each year, the equivalent of nearly 200m barrels of oil.

A move to the cloud in the US would deliver CO_2 reductions of 85.7m tonnes each year, the equivalent of nearly 200m barrels of oil

That translates into energy savings for US businesses of $12.3bn in the next ten years if they adopt cloud services. The Verdantix research predicts that the financial benefits from energy reduction and increased IT efficiency in 2011 alone would reach $824m by the end of the year in the US.

Meanwhile market research firm Pike Research has predicted that cloud computing will lead to a 38% reduction in worldwide data centre energy expenditures by 2020. Microsoft too has said that the cloud can cut energy consumption and carbon emissions by 30% or more, as the scale and use of virtualisation in the cloud just makes computing more efficient, while computer makers are busy making components such as memory and processes more efficient too.

The Verdantix survey was sponsored by the Carbon Disclosure Project – an

organisation with a vested interest in promoting green measures. And it wasn't long before dissenters were rounding on the research findings and finding flaws in the argument.

What's the energy source?

One of the main critics of the survey, GreenMonk analyst Tom Raftery, pointed that there had been some rather dubious assumptions. "The mistake here is presuming a direct relationship between energy and carbon emissions. While this might seem like a logical assumption, it is not necessarily valid," he wrote.

"If I have a company whose energy retailer is selling me power generated primarily by nuclear or renewable sources for example, and I move my applications to a cloud provider whose power comes mostly from coal, then the move to cloud computing will increase, not decrease, my carbon emissions."

providers have indeed been rather secretive about their operations, and to try to get an idea of how energy efficient their servers are would prove to be impossible. But data centre specialists themselves – those that host many clients – are currently vying with each other for the accolade of running the world's greenest facilities, with all sorts of design and supply innovations in the way they are built, located and fuelled.

The problem is that even with an overall rating for the efficiency of data centres, the actual usage of a set of servers by a client is much more difficult to assess, and detailed breakdown of the rating by factors such as the energy type can make comparisons less valid.

Location, location...

A good case in point has been an argument made by Greenpeace about a data centre run by Facebook in Oregon, which takes much of its power from coal-fired sources. But in fact it is said to be one of the world's more efficient facilities, because the cool climate in the state allows it to run without mechanical chillers, one of the biggest energy hogs in a data centre.

One organisation that is trying to improve the way in which sustainable computing is reported is the Green Grid, a non-profit consortium of end-users, policy makers, technology providers, facility architects and utility companies looking to improve the efficiency of data centres.

Ali Moinuddin at data centre player, Interxion, is also the European communications committee co-chair of the Green Grid and is aware that there needs to be a better standard of assessment. "The green data centre is at the heart of the whole movement towards sustainable computing. We need

This is the key to many of the arguments: what is the source of the power that is driving those data centres? It was a question raised by Greenpeace in 2010 when it published a report, 'How dirty is your data?', pointing out that there were serious concerns about some of the big players in cloud computing.

Gary Cook, the lead author of that report, said that the problem was the lack of transparency from some of the cloud companies – the secretive nature of firms such as Google and Microsoft has made it difficult to assess the claims they make. He agreed, however, that data centre and server design innovation can greatly improve efficiency and reduce overheads in energy demand and that more in the sector were comfortable with sharing best-practice data, but that without more transparency, such efforts were not worth much.

Cook has a point and some cloud

Who's the greenest of them all?

The ultimate in green data centres could be Icelandic cloud provider, GreenQloud, which uses geothermal energy to power its data centre, with a lot of hydroelectric power thrown in for good measure.

Of course, there aren't many cloud providers that are sitting in a geographic region with millions of litres of naturally heated water on tap. The company uses 100% renewable energy drawn from the Icelandic grid, which is 30% geothermal and 70% hydro.

CEO Eirikur Hrafnsson says that data centres that claim to be green base the claim on spurious reasoning. "When big players talk about their 'greenness' all they are saying is that their data centres are now more efficient in cooling IT equipment. Energy efficiency of data centres and servers cannot keep up with future energy needs and be effective in reducing carbon dioxide emissions. We need to change the energy sources to renewables; it's that simple."

And in a lesson to other providers, the company records all energy use and carbon emissions made by each customer and makes the data freely available to them.

There are certainly other providers that would claim equal credentials with GreenQloud. In the UK, Capgemini's Merlin data centre, in Swindon, is said to be setting a global standard for energy efficiency, with a power usage effectiveness (PUE) rating of just 1.08 (1 would be perfect). Next Generation Data (NGD) Europe, based in Newport, Wales, is claiming to be the first in Europe to run on 100% renewable energy. And Telehouse takes waste heat from a centre in London's East End to pipe hot water to 1,000 local homes, free of charge.

to move beyond just considering power usage effectiveness [PUE – a standard metric for data centres], to carbon usage effectiveness (CUE) and water usage effectiveness (WUE)," he says (water is often used for cooling).

"It makes environmental and business sense to evaluate these metrics. Now the Green Grid has developed the Data Center Maturity Model that sets goals for improving energy efficiency and sustainability across all aspects of the data centre."

Meanwhile, there is a range of questions for a company interested in cloud and green issues to ask a provider:
• What's the energy source of the data centre?

The Green Grid has developed a model that has clear goals for improving energy efficiency

• What metrics does it use to measure energy efficiency?
• What measures has it taken to reduce power consumption?
• What temperature does it run its data centre at?
• If the cloud provider describes itself as green, what criteria has it deployed (planting a few trees outside isn't going to cut it)?
• What information does it provide to its own customers when it comes to energy consumption?

Energy consumption has really only been debated for a few years now, so it's not surprising that there's confusion around. But it's not an issue that's going to go away – a lot of companies are interested in energy saving measures and cloud providers are going to have to get used to the idea of being more open. ∎

Unlocking your organisational talent

Human resources could be one of the most important cloud applications, thanks to its key organisational role, says **Billy MacInnes**

ADOPTING CLOUD SYSTEMS holds the promise of giving HR executives access to systems that enable them to improve their roles by applying a more analytical and strategic approach to their work. It also gives them a new way meet changes in the business. The increasing adoption of mobile technology and mobile working practices in many companies, for example, is putting an emphasis on employee self-service and accessibility that is often easier to deliver from a cloud-based system than an onsite one.

Businesses are evolving and adopting new working practices and styles, putting pressure on HR to meet and support those changes. With budgetary limitations on IT expenditure, cloud software can be an attractive way of keeping pace with such changes without being constrained by in-house IT.

There's no doubt this is a welcome development. A global survey of more than 200 HR executives by Saugatuck Technology, a cloud consultancy, identified significant limitations in the effectiveness of their existing systems to meet their priorities for the organisation. The survey identified a number of areas HR executives were most concerned about their ability to fulfil:

- Acquiring and retaining key talent
- Developing key talent
- Aligning employee performance with business results and compensation
- Building leadership capabilities
- Supporting organisational innovation and change.

When they were asked to rank the ability of their HR systems to deliver these priorities, it became clear the systems did not measure up as well as they would like. In most cases, there was a difference of 30 points or more

between what they wanted to do for the business and what they could do with the systems. A more recent survey returned to the same issues and found, if anything, that the gap is getting worse in some areas, such as acquiring and retaining key talent, developing key talent and building leadership capabilities.

All of which suggests HR professionals would like systems that do a better job of supporting them in fulfilling their objectives for the business. Cloud software could help to bridge the gap. If the cloud means they are no longer hamstrung by the performance constraints that affect their in-house IT resources, HR professionals should be better placed to concentrate on strategic issues such as talent management, building leadership capabilities and supporting organisational innovation and change.

The security objection

But one big objection is of course security. A specialist provider of cloud-based human resources (HR) software, HR Locker, recently noted how the issue of hosting HR data was raised as a security concern during a customer meeting. So the customer was asked where the company's existing HR software was installed and was shown a server in the corner of the office: "It was accessible to everybody and there were four USB ports staring invitingly out at us."

The HR Locker team asked whether the customer felt this was secure and the reply came back that he wasn't sure because "the IT guy" looked after it. It then emerged that the company had employed three of these "IT guys" in as many years.

While this anecdote concerns one company, it's probably indicative of HR ▶

operations in many organisations. How or why should anyone in HR know where the HR data is stored and how secure or not it is? That's the responsibility of the IT guy.

This level of ignorance about the security of data internally is not confined to HR but very likely applies to most, if not all, functions of the business. But data security is a major concern when it comes to the adoption of cloud computing, most particularly when it applies to employee information.

A recent Cloud Industry Forum survey found that when it came to using cloud services, respondents were most reluctant about moving employee information to the cloud, ahead even of accounts and financial data services. The survey also revealed that data security (64% of respondents) and data privacy (62%) were the most significant concerns about the adoption of cloud in their business.

Debunking the objection

This highlights what could be an intriguing contradiction in the shift to cloud computing, namely that one of the most prominent causes of anxiety in any potential adoption of cloud-based software may also be one of the strongest benefits it can deliver. HR Locker, for example, uses Microsoft's $500m data centre outside Dublin to host its service, which provides much greater resilience and data security than anything its customers might have sitting in a corner.

But if suppliers are confident enough to use hosted providers to deliver their products and services, shouldn't customers feel the same? HR and payroll services provider, Cintra, recently announced that its Cintra iQ offering would be hosted by the Cloud Computing

Centre. Why? "Initially, we tried to host Cintra iQ ourselves," says CEO Carsten Staehr, "but our on-premise solution demanded huge upfront costs to purchase the required equipment, build the infrastructure, add the necessary disaster recovery capabilities and maintain the necessary high levels of data security to store our clients' sensitive HR and payroll data."

All of the reasons cited by Staehr for opting to use the Cloud Computing Centre as a host apply equally to HR and IT departments. Removing or assuaging concerns about security is one of the ways in which the cloud can help HR professionals to concentrate more on the core functions of their job. And as we

personal development objectives onto a single system. But rather than going for one of the larger, well-known enterprise suppliers, it opted for a cloud approach with US provider SuccessFactors. The system covers more than 400,000 employees in 190 countries – so the size claim is well justified.

SuccessFactors published research last year that claimed businesses that took a strategic approach to HR, using systems that capture, measure and present information for analysis about the workforce, outperformed the average. It found companies that benefited from this better business intelligence increased the time they spent on strategic priorities by 40% and project completion rose by 67% through better understanding of their talent and putting the right people on the right projects.

The largest cloud computing deployment in the world is at Siemens – its human capital management system

have seen, despite professed concerns about security, most parts of the business are completely unaware of the level of security (or lack thereof) currently being provided in-house.

HR has the biggest cloud

And if HR executives want reassurance that cloud is not just pie in the sky, they can look to the fact that the largest cloud computing deployment in the world is at Siemens – its human capital management system.

When the company set out to align its human resources operations more closely with the strategic objectives of the business, Siemens decided to standardise all its global recruitment and

The larger operators are starting to get in on the act too. In a recent interview with *eCRMGuide.com*, Gretchen Alarcon, vice president of Oracle Fusion HCM strategy, revealed that HCM (human capital management) and CRM (customer relationship management) have been drawing the most interest from customers looking for cloud apps. She also highlighted the better business intelligence provided by these types of systems, which could be used to enhance the work of the HR department.

That, surely, is the heart of the matter: if they can use systems to deliver better intelligence about the business, HR departments can strengthen their role within an organisation and enhance their effectiveness. ∎

SUPPLY CHAIN
a hotspot for the cloud

Because the supply chain involves a lot of fast moving complexity it will benefit greatly from the cloud, as **Billy MacInnes** explains

ONE OF THE MOST important processes in business – and one tailor-made for the cloud – is the supply chain, which has become more complex and turbulent in recent years. Manufacturers have been among the first sectors to act to make their businesses more 'agile' in the face of difficulties in forecasting demand and avoiding stockpiling products that aren't selling, while pressures on the supply chain itself have intensified as

manufacturing has been outsourced to different partners, often in the Far East, bringing added complexity to transport and logistics.

In turn, with so many companies being called on to provide different links in the overall supply chain for a product or service and engaging with it at different points, the pressure has grown on systems to be able to handle and interact with a diversity of suppliers or sub-suppliers.

IT solutions have typically been deployed to make the supply chain more dynamic and to make engagement with the different links in the chain less complex. In 2010, analyst firm Gartner published a survey entitled 'Significant

benefits realised with supply chain management in the cloud', which found that 95% of those surveyed were either using or considering using cloud-based supply chain applications. It found 52% were using cloud or software-as-a-service for CRM, 44% for supply chain execution, 43% for supply chain planning, 43% for B2B/B2C e-commerce, 42% for ERP (enterprise resource planning) and 39% for sourcing and procurement.

In all those areas, another third or so of respondents were evaluating using cloud technology. The major focus was on partner applications that addressed the connectivity and collaboration requirements when processes are

extended to "the trading partner ecosystem". Gartner suggests this is not surprising because companies have spent billions on financial ERP systems that were designed mainly to provide visibility internally. One company told Gartner it was attracted to the cloud-based approach because it was "tired of the long installations of ERP and upgrades when other businesses are reaping value such as quicker time to productivity, greater return on investment and lower costs".

This comment highlights the

> **Pressure has grown on systems to handle and interact with a diversity of suppliers or sub-suppliers**

Cloud computing systems could lead to a revolution in the way supply chain services are provided

disruptive force cloud computing is expected to unleash on many areas of the business landscape, including the supply chain. For example, start-up companies could disrupt the established landscape without significant investment in infrastructure, and new competitive threats will emerge to existing players. Product and service lifecycles will be shortened further, forcing companies with infrastructure-intensive supply chains, such as the company quoted by Gartner, to add cloud-based supply chain solutions to enhance their competitiveness.

Potential problem areas in using cloud computing in supply chain management are pretty much the same as they are for any area of the business. In a recent article, supply chain experts at Accenture suggest companies may have established sophisticated supply chain management systems to give them a competitive edge against competitors, but cloud computing relies on applications and processes that are not customised. It's up to companies to decide how those cloud applications and processes can deliver.

Of course, cloud computing makes it easier for other companies involved in the supply chain to engage with different links in the chain and access systems without major upheaval to their own processes or additional costs to make them compatible. Sharing a common platform means there are no concerns that a supplier may be providing access to its internal IT to a partner that could be a competitor tomorrow. Standardised applications and processes should also strip away much of the technical support and maintenance requirements associated with bespoke systems.

Again there are potential pitfalls as not many companies own or operate their entire supply chain internally, so any decision about using cloud technology is likely to involve multiple partners. The Accenture experts believe this could create "complexities and sensitivities between the participating organisations". But it may also help remove some of the existing complexities in their current supply chain.

Additionally, if those organisations engage with other businesses, it would make life a lot simpler and more flexible if those engagements could take place using cloud-based systems. According to Accenture, adoption of cloud computing systems could "lead to a revolution in the way more supply chain services are provided" by supplanting the current contracted outsourcing model with more flexible, transaction-based models.

This should lead to a model based on flexible collaboration rather than a more formal, rigid, top-down approach. The issue at the moment is how willing companies are to take this route and how quickly they do it. Michael Higgins, senior vice president for IT at Advanced Innovations, an electronics supply chain specialist, is someone who has already made the shift to the cloud. He believes anybody can do it "if they are willing to put the effort in and to overcome the typical fear, uncertainty and doubt".

And Advanced Innovations didn't change its ERP system: it simply deployed it in Amazon's cloud platform. This has made access to the firm's systems "more robust and available to our partners", enhancing ability to sit between customers and the supply chain. The company uses the Oracle E-Business Suite but has written its own web services platform, which has made it easier, for example, for a small transistor maker in China with a laptop to deal with the company through a browser. "Our philosophy is if you can buy a book from Amazon.com, you can manage your supply chain with us," Higgins adds.

He argues the cloud is a "brilliant platform on which to build standards", adding that "the days of bespoke business processes are hopefully drawing to an end". He believes the cloud could be a big advantage for 'tier two' players. "Players like us are leading larger players into the next generation supply chain," he comments. ■

Preparing for the cloud

- Decide which processes can be provided by a cloud-based supplier and which need to be retained in-house
- Work to a detailed return on investment and risk analysis with prospective suppliers to quantify anticipated benefits based on total cost of ownership
- Agree definitions for success: in addition to cost, include areas such as flexibility, scalability and speed to market
- Keep up to speed with developments in the cloud computing market
- Collaborate with supply chain partners and involve them in decision making
- Evaluate frequently to ensure the hoped for benefits are being achieved

Hotspots for the supply chain

- **Planning and forecasting** – capturing spend data, performing basic analytics, planning manufacturing runs and executing statistical demand forecasts
- **Logistics** – applications such as network strategy, inventory management, warehousing and transportation are appearing; global trade compliance, replenishment planning, order processing, transportation load building, fleet management and transportation route planning are likely candidates
- **Sourcing and procurement** – the cloud gives a great opportunity to cut the total cost of ownership, as cloud tools are inherently collaborative and accessible
- **Service and spare parts management** – many companies underperform in this area, despite their often high contribution to the bottom line. Tools such as warranty validation are available now, and applications for returns processing, inventory pooling and distribution are on their way, says Accenture

SOURCE: ACCENTURE. SEE ALSO ITS PAPER, 'SIX QUESTIONS EVERY SUPPLY CHAIN EXECUTIVE SHOULD ASK ABOUT CLOUD COMPUTING'

A great lead for marketing

Cloud-based systems for marketing functions are booming but marketers have much to do still in integrating data, finds **Graham Jarvis**

ALTHOUGH MARKETING (and its counterpart, sales) have traditionally been among the last functions to receive the full attention of the IT department, the rise of the multichannel world, in which customers are much more in the driving seat, has elevated marketers in the pecking order. Not only do they have more budget to spend, but it's an area where they often have a good deal of autonomy on buying decisions, especially now the cloud is opening up applications to non-technical audiences.

Applications that are on the agenda include marketing automation solutions to track marketing campaigns, webinar and web conferencing services such as WebEx, as well as the various array of social media and direct mail and email management tools. A key driver is that today's online world allows marketers to track almost everything a customer does, because so much is now done on the Internet.

But it is not so easy to find out what applications are likely to be the best fit for an organisation. It's important to think about which cloud and on-premise solutions will improve a marketer's ability to increase an organisation's sales, customer loyalty, revenue and profitability, with particular attention to company priorities, which are likely to include customer retention in current tough trading conditions.

Analyst firm Gartner has a good picture of the most popular cloud-based and on-premise marketing solutions. It regularly produces 'magic quadrants' to analyse where certain vendors and their

'best of breed' products are positioned in the market, including quadrants for 'CRM multichannel campaign management' and 'social CRM' (CRM being customer relationship management, of course).

There is a huge choice of CRM software and the term can mean many things to different marketers, but marketing does need a wide range of tools to fulfil many activities, such as email marketing, social CRM, search engine marketing, mobile marketing, social media, e-commerce, customer services and lead generation.

"If you look at Gartner's Magic Quadrants, you will see that on-premise

solutions are best of breed for multi-channel campaign management, and so you would look at systems from companies such as Unica, SAS and Teradata," says Laurence Buchanan, head of CRM at Cap Gemini. These top systems are though mainly aimed at enterprise customers, and there is now a great choice of cloud systems that cater for many niche marketing functions and also integrated solutions – but integration does remain a big challenge.

Why the cloud is vital

According to Arthur Sweetzer, chief marketing officer at 89 Degrees, a US marketing agency, "many marketing executives are struggling to gather and leverage marketing intelligence across disparate addressable marketing channels", and only a third of marketers have integrated their CRM systems into operational marketing systems such as profile- and behaviour-driven email.

He gives four reasons why cloud systems can accelerate time to market, promote relevance to prospects, and improve marketing revenue by as much as a third over a year. First, as few have integrated the marketing 'data warehouse' with email marketing applications, he suggests using a cloud marketing intelligence database instead, and second, the sheer speed of getting such a cloud system running means that disparate data silos can quickly be brought together.

Then Sweetzer notes that marketers can pick and choose the functions they need much more easily from cloud providers than from traditional managed services companies, and finally that a key goal is to look at the insight that centralising multichannel marketing data can give.

"Cloud based marketing can help you ▶

navigate successfully through the sea of data smarter, faster, and at a lower cost than ever before," he says.

Cloud-based categories

Here's a listing of current cloud marketing categories and a brief selection of providers.

- **CRM solutions:** Whenever one mentions cloud-based CRM, the

---

Top marketing buying tips

Before marketers rush out to buy any of these solutions, and considering that there are so many different cloud software offerings on the market, take note of these tips:

- Don't be blinded by the features of any given solution, but make sure that it meets your key business requirements
- Be clear about how you are going to measure the success of implementing cloud-based marketing solutions
- Ensure that each solution is integrated to capture customer data and track online behaviour for CRM purposes
- Recognise that the market has changed, and how people buy has altered too: solutions that were effective in the past might not be today
- Look for cloud-based solutions that are affordable, easy to use and adopt
- Invest in quality training and make sure that you try out and test the cloud-based applications before you are committed to them
- Do it because it will drive benefits like being able to react more quickly to changes in the market, reduce the time-to-market of a campaign, and lead to revenue growth
- Get going now. There's no point in waiting as the technologies to make marketing more efficient and effective are there, and wasting six months testing each application won't help anyone, so learn by trial and error

---

company that is first suggested is Salesforce.com. There are many others now, such as Microsoft Dynamics CRM, and NetSuite, RightNow and SugarCRM offer alternatives to the larger CRM players. Salesforce.com has a huge range of add-on applications from third parties that can meet almost any marketing need.

- **Email marketing:** Two of the leaders in this field are ExactTarget and Responsys, and most of these solutions are now cloud-based. ExactTarget has grown on the back of Salesforce.com, offering high-volume email management solutions.
- **Data quality and marketing automation:** Marketo, Eloqua, Aprimo and Informatica are all recommended.
- **Web and data analytics:** SAS is often the first to be mentioned in most conversations about analytics, but marketers might also wish to look at the cloud-based solutions of QlikView, Google, Microsoft, Yahoo and others. Google tends to lead the market whenever it comes to cloud-based web analytics. Omniture is a company said to offer a strong web analytics, testing and targeting tool.
- **Business information:** Hoover and OneSource are commended as being best of breed by Fergus Gloster, managing director of the EMEA region at Marketo.
- **Social media management:** Radian6 was recently acquired by Salesforce.com, and so has a strong position in the market. "If you have a look at the role of managing social interaction to find out what's happening in the social media sphere, it probably has the best platform for doing that," says Gloster. The key task is to be able to integrate CRM solutions, for example, with Facebook, Twitter, Linkedin and other

What organisations use CRM for - and what they add on

What do people use CRM for?

Overwhelmingly, of course, it's for contact management (94% in a recent survey). The top applications/areas are (in order):

- Contact management
- Opportunity management
- Sales analytics/forecasting
- Telesales/inside sales
- Customer service
- Lead generation
- Mobile working
- Territory management.

Add-ons that companies are using (in order):

- Customer record lists/data cleaning service
- Customer reference system
- Customer satisfaction surveys/monitoring
- Extra reporting/analytics
- Business intelligence services/ market research
- Call centre systems
- Relationship mapping tools
- Web analytics.

SOURCE: INSTITUTE OF SALES AND MARKETING MANAGEMENT/ ONESOURCE CRM SURVEY 2011

social media platforms to create meaningful online conversations and relationships with customers.

- **Multichannel campaign management:** Eloqua, Marketo, Responsys, Alterian and ExactTarget can also be found within Gartner's magic quadrant. Cap Gemini, for example, is working with Royal Mail, which has decided to use Eloqua. The reasons behind the choice include speed of deployment, ease of use, its range and mix of capabilities and ability to drive consumer and business-to-business campaigns. Another driver was the ability to integrate Eloqua with Salesforce.com.

- **Inbound marketing:** Laurence Buchanan suggests that HubSpot is a solution that's worth examining here.

- **Marketing research:** Clive Longbottom, services director at analyst research firm, Quocirca, suggests Survey Monkey and Google Forms as options here. Another offering is Confirmit.

- **Web-based audio and videoconferencing:** Two big offerings are Cisco WebEx and Microsoft Live Meeting. Both allow companies to reduce the need to travel, and they can

be used by marketers to hold webinars and meetings with colleagues and customers from any location in the world. These tools are available in the cloud. Another big player is Citrix.

- **Customer reference management:** This is a growing area that aims to standardise customer success stories and related material to help salespeople with replicable sales processes. Providers include a US firm called Boulder Logic.

By considering also the top tips (see box), and working collaboratively with IT, marketers should be able better to prove their value to their organisations – it has long been difficult to show return on investment from marketing, but cloud tools should improve this aim.

Certainly, with the cloud, marketers can achieve many of their objectives today without waiting for a suitable solution to be developed for them by their IT departments.

Start with a budget in mind, but don't overly focus on cost; the cloud is scalable, and even small organisations can gain access to secure and scalable enterprise level applications. ∎

What not to do in public

There is a lot of industry hype on what we should do with the new powers offered by public cloud computing. **Adrian Bridgwater** provides a reality check

IF WE CAN AGREE on what not to do inside the cloud computing model of IT delivery we should be steered towards areas where the cloud does excel. So here are ten issues to consider in your cloud computing strategy as exceptions to the rule of the new order in IT.

1 HEAVYWEIGHT INPUT/ OUTPUT APPLICATIONS

Let's start with a good solid truism. Software systems such as databases that require high performance in terms of communications traffic are, generally speaking, not best suited to shared public clouds. There is always the potential with any shared infrastructure that you will be competing for the same hardware performance.

2 COMPLEX, SENSITIVE MISSION-CRITICAL DATA

A software application that is built around the need to collate and manage sensitive data is not best suited to shared multi-tenancy cloud computing. Yes the public cloud is very safe and there are security controls and firewalls that will provide customers with adequate levels of protection, but you will be introducing additional risk that could be mitigated

simply by keeping the data in question on a private server.

3 CONSISTENT 24x7 WORKLOAD

If an application workload is flat and unchanging, then public cloud computing is hardly a best practice choice for maximising financial benefits.

According to Nigel Beighton, chief technology officer at cloud infrastructure player, Rackspace: "Public cloud computing, with utility PAYG [pay as you go] charging offers immense flexibility, but if your workload is constant and unvarying then the 'usage charge' model is unlikely to be advantageous."

He adds: "A flat and unchanging IT requirement logically means that you can buy the appropriate amount of on-premise hardware to fit the bill. Using the cloud in this instance is not necessarily a problem, but it is really not prudent or efficient. For example, if you know you need a car seven days a week, you don't go out and hire one every morning now do you?

"It is the same concept. The cloud is there to help cope with unpredictability and changeability, not computing scenarios characterised by stability."

4 STRINGENT AUDIT and COMPLIANCE

Some data regulations and compliancy rulings require the auditing of where a customer's data and processes actually sit. By this we really mean 'where' – street address, floor, server room number, blade rack and disk partition. But the public cloud is a virtual world, where it is often not possible to identify (or the public cloud provider cannot disclose) which physical server or disk that hosts processes and data.

5 A SOFTWARE LICENCE BRICK WALL

It's a plain and simple fact that far too many software licences have still not evolved to accommodate cloud computing. Nathan Marke, chief technology officer of 2e2, an IT services provider, suggests that existing maintenance, support and managed service contracts can act as a barrier to moving IT services into the cloud. He cites recent research that found that 57% of organisations said such contracts ▶

would lead to delays in deploying some cloud services and Marke says that this isn't surprising considering that often organisations will have three to five year fixed-term contracts.

"Organisations do need to be wary of migrating to the cloud when they may still be committed to legacy contracts that they won't now use," he says.

6 CLOUD GROWTH IS HORIZONTAL, NOT VERTICAL

Applications that can only scale from increasing the performance of the server they are running on are not really able to exploit the fundamental benefit of cloud, which is horizontal scale – we need the right vehicle for the job in hand. "Don't use a helicopter when you need a Hercules," says Stephen Eveleigh, product marketing manager at Star, an on-demand computing and communications company.

"Multi-tenanted/public cloud has its place, but will not meet all business requirements," he says. "Some applications need to be integrated and tailored to company needs – with a dedicated, private cloud you can achieve this. The new breed of cloud-savvy IT directors understand business requirements and make business-focused decisions on whether public, private or hybrid are the right choice for each application."

Michael Newberry, Windows Azure lead at Microsoft UK, points out that since multicore computer processor became mainstream, performance growth has generally come from the adoption of concurrency. Applications that cannot scale concurrently, those that are 'single-threaded' for example, will not run faster with more cores regardless of whether those cores are

on-premise or in the cloud.

He adds: "But scalability is not the only benefit of cloud. There are other good reasons, such as rapid provisioning or agility, for moving something into the cloud even if the application itself does not scale linearly."

7 AVOID CLOSED SOURCE CLOUDS

Evangelists of open source IT argue that the core issue of escalating expenses associated with any vendor is inherently caused by lock-in to that provider. If we accept this as true, then there are ramifications for the cloud, says Aram Kananov, a product marketing manager at open source specialist, Red Hat.

"We see such tactics adopted by a majority of vendors that base their technology on closed proprietary software and proprietary standards," he says. "This is why all major players in the emerging cloud space often base their 'stacks' on open source software and open standards to prevent any particular vendor dictating their future technology decisions. This is also the reason why the vast majority of public cloud service providers run their infrastructures on the Linux operating system. Indeed, the new emerging cloud applications are extensively using open source software."

8 CRITICAL SEPARATION SITUATION

Just as application performance needs to exploit the inherent cloud feature of 'scale through replication', so does application resiliency. A single instance on any public cloud can be vulnerable to all the aspects of a shared public service, as Star's Steve Eveleigh comments. "A cloud-savvy IT director will work with cloud services providers who 'get this' and will work to mitigate this risk."

9 STANDARD BUILD GOOD, CUSTOM BUILD BAD

Cloud computing does not necessarily suit a computing environment where a customer has an extremely complex 'custom-build' job for certain software applications. "Cloud computing environments have much lower running costs in part because they are standardised," says Microsoft's Michael Newberry. "So applications that require non-standard hardware will not necessarily benefit from the same economies of scale.

"Software designers need to consider extensibility and configurability when they design applications so software can service individual customer requirements without necessarily needing to be a custom build. This enables them to take advantage of standardised infrastructures."

10 CRUMBLING FOUNDATIONS, PALTRY PORTABILITY

The cloud may be 'up there' and the new computing resources it offers may be strong, but we still need to have strong IT foundations on the ground if we are to look skywards. This means that it's not a great idea to move to the cloud if your underlying network is a flaky, archaic collection of resources built around legacy applications that are closely tied to obsolete equipment – and disentangling them might be a tough ask.

If you've got a Roman ruin here on Earth, then not even Jupiter, Zeus and Apollo can get you into the cloud. Equally, if your legal team has not been able to ratify the holy scriptures of your cloud agreement's small print, then you may well find that your IT department quickly becomes a bunch of non-believers.

Analogies aside, the small print governs the precision-engineered elements of whether a cloud migration with enjoy fluid portability – and at this time, we are still in need of hard and fast standards. From portability of cloud-to-cloud applications, to bringing cloud-based workloads back into the enterprise data centre if circumstances change, portability is paramount.

The weakest link: how secure is the cloud?

Cloud security is the number one concern for most users, and as **Adrian Bridgwater** discusses, we may have to wait for trust to build

WE CURRENTLY APPEAR to be at a stage where confidence in cloud computing security is (if you believe the surveys) still very much in question. This perception appears to be driven at least in part by the 'distance' between the customer and the cloud provider – inevitably, having much of your vital IT applications and data not under your own roof does raise concerns. But this does not inherently mean that cloud application security risks are more difficult to curtail than running all your systems in-house.

So where should we draw the lines around cloud applications and data security? A good starting point is a Ponemon Institute cloud security survey, which found that only 36% of the 925 respondents questioned believed their organisations are vigilant in conducting audits or assessments of cloud computing resources prior to deployment. More specifically, the survey found that IT practitioners (at all levels) lack confidence in their employer's ability to secure data and applications deployed in cloud computing environments (especially public clouds).

The root of the problem

So it is important to stand back at this point and question whether it is the cloud that is at risk of being insecure, or is it really the application itself that needs to be locked down? The greatest data risks to any organisation come from within; susceptibility to data damage from employees' own use of a network, whether via premeditated or accidental action, remains the biggest security issue of all.

This 'insider threats' message is repeated by anti-virus vendors again and again; enterprise-level applications may be inherently insecure, whether they sit on the corporate network, in a private cloud data repository of some making, or ultimately, out in the public cloud. The cloud itself is not insecure: what you put in the cloud may well be insecure. If you accept this basic truism, then we can move on.

And if we have been this worried about cloud security, then surely there should have been some kind of governing body established to oversee cloud security fundamentals? This is of course what the Cloud Security Alliance (CSA) sets out to do. The CSA's Certificate of Cloud Security Knowledge (CCSK) aims to set a professional bar for what we tend to call 'practitioners', but we should perhaps just call users, software developers and IT managers.

The Cloud Security Alliance describes itself as a not-for-profit organisation with a mission to promote the use of best practices for providing security

assurance within cloud computing. The organisation is clearly having some influence on the industry; its corporate member list doubles as a handy who's who of the cloud industry, and this year's CSA Summit drew in Vivek Kundra, chief information officer at the White House, as a keynote speaker.

What can companies do to stay secure?

But at a lower level than industry body edicts and infrastructure standards, what kind of thing can companies to do address security issues in the cloud? First, no right-minded commercial entity should approach the deployment of any application (from a simple email client application to a mission-critical database) without security software controls in place.

Encryption layers, firewalls, anti-malware suites and spam filters all have a purpose – but this is not the place for a complete list of security controls. So take it as read that if these protection mechanisms are needed on the ground in your organisation, then they are needed in the cloud in equal measure.

At a deeper level still, fine-grained access controls can help. This is the level at which users should only be able to

►

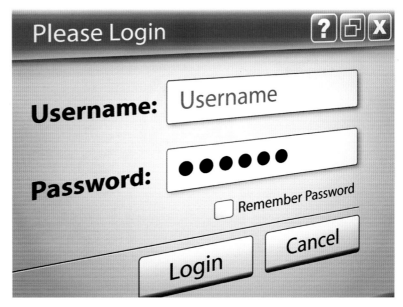

access the 'rows' or table values in (for instance) a cloud application database that they are authorised to have access to. For example, a sales rep using a cloud-based application and its corresponding data store may only be able to view their own sales – and not the figures of their colleagues or their department or company as a whole.

The vendor's viewpoint

Cloud providers themselves are of course best placed to handle customers' security concerns because they themselves sit closest to the data. In an effort to share some of this 'proximity', cloud infrastructure provider Rackspace recently launched its so-called 'extreme' mission critical cloud offering, known as Critical Sites. This service is said to drill into the

application layer to provide real-time visibility of clients' most important websites and applications.

What this means is that customers will get performance management tools and a 'web-scale' engineering team on a five-minute 'notification of events' service level agreement (SLA) to address sensitivities. When cloud users want security analysis reviews for applications, infrastructure and architecture, with this service they can have it. As the cloud computing evolves, this kind of SLA is likely to become increasingly prevalent.

Echoing this 'proximity' message is Michael Newberry, product manager for Windows Azure at Microsoft UK. "Cloud providers uniquely understand their platform and are best placed to describe the controls customers can use to achieve their required level of security, so customers can then determine if the capabilities and controls

> **People have trusted their money to banks for years, but may only have had cloud for months**

are suitable for their own requirements," he explains.

Again resonating with the assertion that the cloud is "only as good as the application", Newberry continues: "While responsibility for compliance with laws, regulations and industry requirements remains with Windows Azure customers, Microsoft's commitment to providing fundamental security capabilities is key to our customers' success with the offering." So the word 'trust' is key.

Taken on trust

We often use the analogy of banking when it comes to cloud security. As individuals, we entrust our money to our bank on the understanding that other customers don't get to see our details and transactions. This is not dissimilar to the cloud model in some ways; we place our data and applications with "reputable" cloud provider brands, safe in the knowledge that these companies will honour the sanctity of the SLA and data privacy agreements that we customers sign.

Whether this trust ever needs to be brought into question is still a moot point for many IT directors who are considering cloud migrations. But as Jon Honeyball, who writes for *Cloud Pro*, has said, people have trusted their money to banks for many years, but may have only had cloud for months in some cases.

As we now move forward, we may need to endure the natural passage of time before we collectively assign the same levels of trust to cloud computing as we might do today to say corporate banking. From this point we may then experience a level where the cloud actually makes data more secure than if left unmanaged. Will this ultimately happen? "It can and it will," is Honeybull's prophecy. ∎

Top five cloud security tips

1 **Encryption equality** – Application encryption on the ground should equal application encryption in the cloud. Firms need to initiate this process by first performing an inventory analysis of all cloud resources to be managed, and then assessing the business risk associated with each element of the IT 'stack'. Appropriate levels of encryption can then be applied.

2 **Mission-critical omissions** – All applications are not the same. So-termed 'extreme' (or high risk) mission-critical cloud-based applications are different, so there will always be some data that you don't host in the cloud. This could be data relating to national security, business intellectual property or sensitive customer account data.

3 **SSL and VPN is the 'ABC'** – Look to see that your cloud provider has basic secure sockets layer (SSL) and virtual private network (VPN) layers in place. This should be among the 'ABC' first principles of cloud security best practice, so that information in transit has a core level of encryption.

4 **Policing policy practice** – Formalised security and access control policies are a prerequisite to using the cloud securely. Whether your firm produces a one-page document or conducts formal in-house training, policy controls are the bedrock of cloud security best practice.

5 **Transparency, clarity and visibility** – Constantly auditing your cloud provider's service for true visibility is crucial. The Ponemon study found that half of all respondents recognise that many cloud resources are not evaluated for security prior to deployment. In practice, the process of pre-evaluation, re-evaluation and audit analysis with a view to achieving application and data transparency, clarity and visibility is essential.

Who's who in cloud computing

There are hundreds of companies active in the cloud computing space – we pick the top movers and shakers in the industry

IT'S IMPOSSIBLE TO LIST all the many companies active in cloud computing – so here's a list that includes most of the big players plus a selection of smaller firms. Cloud providers come in all shapes and sizes, but key categories are:

- Infrastructure players, which provide the data centres and management tools to host public, private and hybrid clouds
- Platform players, which allow many different application vendors to supply a service
- Application software firms, which have cloud-based systems such as sales, accounts and so on
- Operation management providers, which offer services such as remote storage.

Some companies are active in several categories and the lines are blurred in any case – this is one of the fastest ever moving sectors in IT.

Akamai

Akamai is a Hawaiian word meaning intelligent or wise. The company provides a distributed computing platform that mirrors content from customer servers on its global platform of servers. Web Application Accelerator is Akamai's infrastructure-as-a-service offering, designed to speed up the performance of web applications without the client requiring additional infrastructure.

Amazon Web Services

Amazon Web Services was established in 2006 and yes, it's part of the multi-billion dollar online bookseller. In fact, AWS uses Amazon.com's global computing infrastructure – which is the backbone of the retail business and transactional enterprise – to provide scalable and secure cloud computing infrastructure to clients. Amazon is one of the giants in the cloud and its offerings are billed on usage.

- EC2 is an infrastructure-as-a-service offering that stands for Elastic Compute Cloud. It operates on a simple web service interface, which allows clients to obtain and configure capacity readily, and provides developers with tools to build resilient applications.
- S3, or Simple Storage Service, is Amazon's storage offering, and provides a simple web services interface that can be used to store and retrieve any amount of data at any time, from anywhere on the web, using the cloud.
- Elastic Beanstalk is Amazon's deployment and management service. It allows users to quickly deploy and manage applications in Amazon's cloud. Users upload applications and Elastic Beanstalk automatically handles capacity provisioning, load balancing, auto-scaling and application health monitoring.
- AWS CloudFormation gives developers and systems administrators an easy way to create a collection of related Amazon cloud resources and provision them in an orderly and predictable fashion.

Telcos like BT are natural cloud players

Apple
Apple has enjoyed extraordinary success in recent years with the iPhone, iPad and the Mac computer range, and has recently trialled a new cloud offering, not surprisingly named iCloud, which is aimed at consumers and stores music, photos, applications, documents and so

on and makes them available as if they were stored locally.

BeyondTrust
BeyondTrust is an American company specialising in privilege authorisation management, access control and security solutions for virtualisation and cloud computing environments. The company's offerings are designed to strengthen security, drive compliance and eliminate the risk of intentional, accidental and indirect misuse of privileges on desktops and servers.

BT
BT, the major British telecoms company of course, now provides cloud computing services including products such as Salesforce.com and NetSuite. BT's Virtual Data Centre offers a range of cloud capabilities, including both public and private cloud systems.

CA Technologies
CA Technologies is an IT management and software solutions company operating across all IT environments from mainframe to the cloud, including both public and private cloud computing solutions. In 2010, CA Technologies acquired Nimsoft, a provider of IT performance and availability monitoring solutions that can be used in cloud applications.

Canonical
Canonical is a UK software firm that offers cloud computing services through its Ubuntu software, which allows users to create a private cloud within their own IT infrastructure or to deploy a cloud with ▶

one of Canonical's partners, including Amazon, Microsoft and RedHat. It is flexible – enabling customers to switch between clouds – and features frequently updated security procedures.

Cisco

Cisco is a multinational systems company providing communications and networking technology. It's cloud offerings include:

- Secure MultiTenancy – owned collectively by Cisco, VMware and NetApp, this cloud-hosting infrastructure-as-a-service offering uses pre-tested and validated computer 'stacks' and fault-tolerant architecture
- WebEx – Cisco's collaborative suite that combines real-time desktop sharing and phone conferencing, and allows the sharing of documents, presentations and applications across PCs, Macs and mobile devices. Up to six webcams can be streamed at once.

Citrix

Citrix provides cloud services such as server and desktop virtualisation, software-as-a-service, conferencing, open source products and networking. The company has data centres around the world including the UK, India and Australia. It acquired XenSource in October 2007. Citrix OpenCloud is the main cloud computing platform.

CloudShare

Previously known as IT Structures, CloudShare is a California-based cloud provider founded in Israel. It offers a self-service platform that enables organisations to create virtual data centres for a range of business functions including application development and testing, demonstrations, proofs of

CloudShare enables you to create virtual data centres using a self-service platform

concept and IT training and certification. CloudShare Enterprise is the main infrastructure-as-a-service offering, and other products include CloudShare Pro, a free, individual version of the platform that enables individuals and small teams to manage complex virtual IT environments in the cloud.

Commensus

A UK provider of a cloud platform known as C-VIP, which operates across five data centres, three in London, and one each in Paris and Frankfurt. It backs its service with a 99.999% uptime service-level agreement.

Dell

Dell is known mainly as a PC maker, but it also provides cloud computing, consulting and data storage services. Offerings include infrastructure management, virtual integration and mobile management services.

ElasticHosts

ElasticHosts is a London-based cloud provider. The company stands out mainly because it charges by the resources required, such as memory, disk, processor and network, as separate entities, allowing customers to create virtual machines with any configurations they choose. Its scalable infrastructure-as-a-service offerings can run on any OS.

EMC

EMC is a long-standing data management giant that delivers cloud services such as Atmos, a large-scale storage system. It recently announced ProSphere, a storage resource management offering "designed from the ground up specifically to address the rapidly evolving needs of enterprises as they migrate to highly virtualised, cloud-based computing models".

Fasthosts

Fasthosts is a leading UK web hosting and cloud solutions provider. As well as offering a comprehensive range of web hosting, email and server products, Fasthosts is at the forefront of developing innovative cloud solutions for the SME market including virtual servers, software-as-a-service, secure online storage and back-up. Fasthosts developed its own virtual server platform, called DataCenter on Demand, as the foundation of its virtual solutions. This year the company has won the Microsoft Hyper-V Cloud Partner Award 2011 and Microsoft's Hosting Partner of the Year Award.

Fujitsu

Fujitsu is a major provider of IT systems, services and products in the UK. Its infrastructure-as-a-service offering uses secure data centres with the resilience and performance levels required for business systems hosting. Client data is hosted in the original country, maintaining data privacy and legal jurisdiction for business information. Fujitsu's platform-as-a-service offering enables software vendors to reach markets on a pay-per-use basis.

GoGrid

GoGrid is a California-based cloud infrastructure service provider that first began offering cloud solutions in 2008. The company offer cloud solutions hosted by Linux and Windows virtual machines. GoGrid Cloud Storage is a file-level back-up service for Windows and Linux servers.

Google

California-based multinational Google is best-known for its leading search engine but also provides cloud computing solutions and other Internet-based services and products. It was founded in 1998 to "organise the world's information" and runs more than a million servers in its data centres. It operates the well-known Gmail email service, web browser Google Chrome, the Google Talk messaging application and even produces operating systems for mobile telephones.

- Google Apps is the company's software-as-a-service offering, providing customisable versions of Google's own products, including Gmail, Docs, Talk, Google Groups, Sites and Google Calendar. It provides services for business and education (the latter is free).
- Google Cloud Storage enables developers to store and access data on the company's data centre infrastructure. All data is replicated to

Google: a firm that's organised to work in a cloud

multiple US-based data centres, has individual and group-based access controls and key-based authentication.

HP

HP, or Hewlett-Packard, is the world's largest computer maker, producing servers, laptops, mobile phones, printers and scanners, and has entered the cloud market.

• Enterprise Cloud Services-Compute offers computational services using HP's data centres. The service is a pre-built, off-premise cloud designed to run core applications with scalability.

• CloudService Automation is HP's software-as-a-service offering, and offers a package of cloud-building hardware, software and services. It allows systems to be integrated with Enterprise Cloud Service-Compute so users can jump between their private cloud and HP's.

IBM

IBM has joined other well-known IT brands in offering cloud services, such as LotusLive, a cloud-based enterprise networking and collaboration tool integrating email, social networking for business, file sharing, instant messaging and data visualisation, integrated with Skype, LinkedIn and Salesforce.com.

Computing giant IBM has recently launched LotusLive

Intuit

The company produces financial and taxation software to service the small business and the accountancy industry. Its flagship products are Quicken, QuickBooks and TurboTax. Intuit now offers cloud-based versions of its applications.

Iomart

UK firm Iomart has figured highly in global rankings of cloud providers. It offers managed hosting and private/hybrid cloud computing based on its data centre estate in the UK, and runs data centres in London, Maidenhead, Glasgow, Nottingham and Leicester.

Joyent

Founded in 2004 and headquartered in San Francisco, Joyent is a software, virtualisation and IT services company specialising in the cloud. It offers cloud services for large online clients, including social networking site LinkedIn (it was also the original host of Twitter). The company is also active in the online gaming industry.

Microsoft

Microsoft has dominated many aspects of computing and has now entered the cloud with Microsoft Cloud Power, and has a number of software and platform offerings that use familiar Microsoft interfaces:

• Office 365 is an evolution of Microsoft Online Services and combines Microsoft Office with the advantages of the cloud. Users can access email, documents, contacts and calendars from anywhere with an Internet connection

• Windows Azure is both a software and platform service provided on a pay-for-use model. It offers multiple

application development tools, automated service management and a global data centre presence
- Microsoft's Business Productivity Suite delivers the company's familiar suite of services from the cloud, including 25 gigabytes of mailbox storage, and access through a variety of mobile devices to key services such as email, calendar and shared content
- SharePoint is Microsoft's collaboration platform, bringing together familiar Microsoft interfaces and using the cloud to provide a single, integrated location where employees can work with their team members, share knowledge and find organisational resources and information.

Microsoft's Office apps are now making a cloud move

NetSuite
NetSuite is a provider of cloud computing business management software. Key offerings include:
- NetSuite's business software incorporates everything from accounting and financial resource planning (ERP) to customer relationship management (CRM)
- NetSuite OneWorld, a cloud-based on-demand system to deliver real-time global business management and financial consolidation to mid-sized companies with multinational and

multi-subsidiary operations
- SuiteAnalytics, which provides real-time business intelligence using real-time dashboards. It uses the cloud to give real-time views of company performance, finance, sales, marketing and service fulfilment.

Nimbus
Nimbus offers business process management software to help its clients capture, manage and deploy their operational processes and supporting information to their workforce, wherever they are, using the cloud. The company is a Microsoft Gold Certified Partner and a partner with SAP, Oracle and Salesforce.com.

Novell
Novell is a US multinational software and services company that offers platform cloud services, including Cloud Manager, which automates complex provisioning workflows, from requests and approvals to creating and employing new business services, and Cloud Security Service, which improves security if a company uses more than one cloud application, through a secure, single password log-in.

Oracle
Software giant Oracle delivers both private and public cloud computing solutions. Clients pay for what they use and have a choice of deployment models using Oracle's scalable cloud infrastructure. Offerings include:
- Oracle Exalogic Elastic Cloud – a platform for enterprise-wide data centre consolidation on any scale, from small departmental applications to large and demanding mainframe applications
- Oracle On Demand – a flexible deployment model for applications. ▶

Parallels

Parallels provides virtualisation and automation software across all of the main operating systems. The company is working with a group of independent software vendors and service providers to expand their cloud products for customers of all sizes, including helping large companies to develop in-house clouds.

Plan B

Plan B is a specialist IT disaster recovery business based in the UK. It says it provides 'near instant recovery' of working systems on its Rescue Cloud of remote virtual servers.

Rackspace

Rackspace has been hosting website, applications, email servers, security and storage since 2001. It makes a big deal of what it calls the "fanatical support" it offers to customers and has several levels of hosting services in both the public and private clouds. Offerings include:

• Cloud Files, which provides unlimited online storage with easy upload and speedy file transfer
• Cloud Servers, which allow you to choose your own operating system, choose a server size and only pay for what you use
• Cloud Sites, which spreads your traffic across a cluster of servers
• Jungle Disk and Cloud Drive, which allow small business and personal users to securely store, back-up and share files in the cloud at low cost.

Red Hat

Red Hat is an open source and cloud provider which recognises that each client's IT infrastructure is likely to comprise hardware and software from a

Red Hat's Enterprise Virtualisation platform is ideal for heavy demand

variety of vendors. Its philosophy is that you should be allowed to use and manage those assets as one cloud rather than being locked into one vendor and it delivers a number of cloud solutions including its Enterprise Virtualisation platform for businesses with heavy cloud demands.

RightScale

RightScale is a cloud computing management company that offers an automated platform for on-demand cloud services. Products include the Cloud Management Platform for reducing administration and the complexity of managing cloud deployments, while still giving flexibility, control and portability.

Salesforce.com

Salesforce.com specialises in CRM (customer relationship management) applications. It started as a CRM software-as-a-service provider, and has now expanded into the wider cloud and social enterprise arena. Services include:

• Sales Cloud 2, the main CRM cloud application
• Service Cloud 2, a customer service platform

SuccessFactors .

- Chatter, a private social network, like Facebook, which can be used internally in a company
- Force.com, a cloud platform for business applications, allowing developers to create applications that are hosted on Salesforce.com's infrastructure.

Savvis

Savvis offers a flexible, scalable and easy-to-use cloud interface. It provides public and private network connectivity and has 31 data centres across the world, including in Europe, the US and Asia.

Star

UK-based Star was founded in 1995 and pioneered a cloud-based spam and virus scanning system for business email that eventually evolved into MessageLabs, a messaging and web security specialist. An IT and communications services provider, Star offers email, telephony, hosting and networking, and now delivers a range of cloud computing solutions, including WorkLife, which brings together email, telephony, instant messaging, document management, conferencing and collaboration technology.

SunGard Availability Services

The company provides IT operations support including integrated disaster recovery, managed services, IT consulting and business continuity management software. It offers an enterprise-class private cloud service, a back-up service called Replication-as-a-Service, Electronic Vaulting, for encrypted and secure storage of data that links directly to a recovery system, and a cloud-based continuity management solution.

2e2

2e2 describes itself as an IT "lifecycle services" provider, and the UK firm is active in cloud infrastructure deployment. It says: "We believe that various hybrid strategies – marrying existing dedicated IT investments with either public or private cloud technologies – are the inevitable answer for at least the next five years as the cloud market evolves and stabilises. Cloud should mean reduced costs and rapid deployment of innovative applications, but never at the expense of procurement difficulties or piecemeal, indifferent support levels."

Unisys

The company has focused on what it considers to be the three challenges that need to be addressed for cloud computing to be viable, namely security, compliance and application rewrites, and migration. It offers solutions across many business areas including finance, budget planning, HR, payroll, email, collaboration, analytics and data storage. Offerings include Virtual Office-as-a-Service, which provides hosted 'desktops' using Unisys's secure cloud infrastructure on a subscription basis. It is designed to simplify desktop maintenance, reduce support costs and improve security compared with traditional desktop PCs.

VMware

VMware offers virtualisation systems and cloud infrastructure from the desktop to the data centre. The company provides private cloud and public/hybrid cloud solutions with safeguards and governance compliance, and clients can build applications that are portable between the clouds within a common management framework. ■

Glossary to cloud computing terms

Agility
Can refer to faster, simpler steps for provisioning IT and also wider business processes.

CAPEX
Capital expenditure – the traditional way to purchase IT equipment. Large investments are made in one financial year to benefit the business over the lifetime of the hardware which would typically be three to five years. This is in contrast to OPEX.

Cloud
Simply the global internet, the network beyond your own building.

Cloud backup
Backing up data to internet-based storage systems. As well as being a simple way to backup data it has the added benefit of keeping a copy of data offsite. Disadvantages can potentially include the amount of time to backup and restore files, particularly where data changes frequently and internet bandwidth is limited. Zmanda, Carbonite and Mozy provide services in this area.

Cloud broker
An organisation that acts as a liaison between multiple cloud service providers and customers, by selecting the best provider for particular services.

Cloud bursting
Cloud bursting is a common practice within hybrid clouds to provide additional resources to private clouds as and when they're needed

Cloud infrastructure
Consists of servers, storage area networks (SANs), networking components and virtualisation software that combine to provide a fault tolerant, flexible and scalable system. Cloud infrastructures are housed in data centres.

Cloud pyramid
A picture of cloud computing layers by functionality, such as infrastructure, platform and application.

Cloud service provider
A company that provides cloud services over the Internet. Large data centres are used to run applications and store data in fault tolerant configurations. The long list of providers includes Amazon, Google, Microsoft and Salesforce.com.

Cloud storage
Storage of files on Internet based systems. Cloud storage can be used as part of a SaaS solution where the application and storage are both located on the cloud. Another option is to use it as a store for data that can be transferred

+ PUE.
+ Carbon Tax Shell

to or from the local network via a web browser or locally installed application. Companies offering cloud storage solutions include Amazon, Rackspace and Microsoft.

Cloud washing
A tactic by vendors, especially software companies, to rebrand their offerings as cloud computing but without true cloud functionality.

Community cloud
A cloud that is shared by a number of organisations with some common interests and aims.

Data centre
Buildings that house cloud infrastructures including servers, storage systems and networking equipment. Also known as cloud centres.

Elasticity
Cloud computing can scale up and down depending on demand.

Hybrid cloud
A system that uses a combination of private and public clouds.

Internal cloud
See Private cloud.

Infrastructure-as-a-service (IaaS)
A service that provides access to virtual servers. In the case of a public cloud, this service would be hosted by a third party and accessed over the internet. It's important to be aware of licensing implications when using this type of service. Services are normally billed on the consumption of resources such as processor and memory.

Amazon and Rackspace both offer services in this area.

Mash-up
Combining input from multiple sources in a web application.

Multi-tenancy
A single instance of an application used for many customers, with each customer only able to access their own data. Customers may be able to customise aspects of the software for their data, but only within the limitations imposed by the developers.

OPEX
Operational expenditure costs incurred for services within a financial year. As cloud computing is charged on a subscription basis, it marks a shift from CAPEX to OPEX, making budgeting for IT a simpler process.

Platform-as-a-service (PaaS)
Service that provides a framework for developers to run their own code and so can be used for in-house applications. This service is particularly useful when SaaS solutions don't meet the particular business needs. Publishing applications can be greatly speeded up by using this type of service as the hardware and required components are set up by the provider. Services such as Force.com and Microsoft's Windows Azure fit into this category.

Public cloud
Cloud services provided across the internet by third-party providers. Virtualisation technology is used to provide fault tolerant, flexible and expandable systems that can be divided

►

up to provide isolated services on a subscription or usage basis. Companies providing services include Amazon, Salesforce.com, Microsoft and Google.

Private cloud
Uses virtualisation technology to provide similar functionality to a public cloud, but is owned and managed by a single user company. Private clouds may be more suitable than a public cloud when highly sensitive information is stored. The large manufacturers such as Cisco, Dell, HP and IBM provide hardware tailored for private clouds.

Storage area network (SAN)
A fault tolerant storage system that can be accessed through fast network technologies to provide storage to multiple servers. SANs work with virtualisation technology, enabling virtual servers to be moved between physical servers on the fly.

Software-as-a-service (SaaS)
A service that provides access to software across the internet, including office applications, email services and customer relationship management (CRM) systems. The hardware and software is managed by the provider, so there is little requirement for local IT staff for this type of service. Providers include Salesforce.com, NetSuite and Google.

Service level agreement (SLA)
Defines the level of service that a supplier will provide, normally including the percentage of uptime and levels of compensation offered if the supplier doesn't meet their stated figures.

Service provider lock-in
The fear that organisatiions opting for cloud services will be stuck with their original provider and unable to move the data to an alternative provider. Various organisations are looking to create common standards for cloud, the Open Cloud Initiative is probably the best known of these.

Storage service
See Cloud storage.

Utility computing
Providing computing services and charging on a usage basis in much the same way as utility bills. This is a shift from traditional networks where servers need to be purchased and then replaced according to a schedule schedule.

Virtual Private Cloud
Similar to the long-familiar concept of the Virtual Private Network (VPN). Allows organisations to create clouds that look private, from a security point of view.

Virtualisation
Technology used for cloud computing that divides physical servers into multiple smaller virtual servers that each contains their own fully functioning operating system. Virtual servers can be migrated between physical servers and resources, such as processor and memory, and can be increased or decreased as required. VMware, Citrix and Microsoft provide virtualisation solutions. ■